PUMAS

A HISTORY OF ARGENTINE RUGBY

REX GOWAR

POLARIS
PUBLISHING

This edition first published in 2022 by

POLARIS PUBLISHING LTD
c/o Aberdein Considine
2nd Floor, Elder House
Multrees Walk
Edinburgh
EH1 3DX

Distributed by
Birlinn Limited

www.polarispublishing.com

ISBN: 9781913538682
eBook ISBN: 9781913538699

British Library Cataloguing-in-Publication Data
A catalogue record for this book is available on request from the British Library.

Designed and typeset by Polaris Publishing, Edinburgh
Printed in Great Britain by MBM Print, East Kilbride

CONTENTS

INTRODUCTION   v

PREFACE   vii

1: TRIES   1

2: BIRTH   6

3: AMATEUR SPIRIT   16

4: PUMAS PLUS   27

5: SAN ISIDRO   31

6: CASI-SIC   38

7: FRONT ROW   41

8: FRANCE   48

9: THE BRITISH   53

10: PORTA   64

11: GAZELLE   73

12: 'DESAPARECIDOS'   77

13: PUCCIO   83

14: 'THIRD HALF'   88

15: YOUNGEST CAPTAIN   94

16: WORLD CUP   98

17: WYLLIE   109

18: LOFFREDA   119

19: PICHOT   136

20: LEICESTER   154

21: LES   160

22: IRB   173

23: RUGBY CHAMPIONSHIP   176

24: CONTEPOMI   183

25: ATTACK!   192

26: 'EL MAGO'   201

27: SANZAAR   209

28: LEDESMA   214

29: MURDER   221

30: ALL BLACKS   228

31: CARDIFF   233

32: OLYMPICS   239

GLOSSARY   241

ACKNOWLEDGEMENTS   245

BIBLIOGRAPHY   246

INTRODUCTION

IN 2020, THE year of the start of Covid-19, Argentine rugby had some memorable moments and also one of its worst.

The high point came on the playing field with the Pumas' first victory over the world's best team, New Zealand's All Blacks, followed by second place in the three-nation 2020 Rugby Championship after two draws against host team Australia.

A murder tainted rugby in January of the first year disrupted by the pandemic when a group of teenagers, members of a rugby club, kicked a youngster of their age to death outside a seaside resort nightclub.

Rugby in Argentina has struggled with a description as a sport practised by a social elite, with critics pointing to a tribal mix of belonging and superiority to explain cases of gang behaviour among a minority.

A case that became public in the middle of the championship in Australia in November of three members of the Pumas squad who had written racist tweets in their teens a decade earlier exacerbated that view once again.

The vast majority of people involved in Argentine rugby, and its amateur club environment that forms an essential part of their lives, are the first to deplore incidents that give their sport a bad image but have often failed to act to correct it.

There are countless examples of Argentine rugby people overcoming sometimes huge odds, like preparing for the tournament in Australia in isolation and without match practice for a year, and giving in equal measure off the field of play as a community, like taking the game into poor barrios and prisons.

This is the story of their team.

PREFACE

'To be a Puma means being a true rugby player in a much broader sense than the game itself. It is an expression of such values as the friendship, honesty, commitment and responsibility required in any activity we undertake.'
Marcelo Loffreda

THE OUTSTANDING CHARACTERISTIC of Argentina's rugby team, Los Pumas, is to have punched above their weight, almost always. They are driven by a passion for their sport and for the sky blue and white colours they wear.

They sing their national anthem more fervently than any other team as they pump themselves up for matches in which they have invariably been the underdogs when facing the world's top teams: the British, Irish and French and Australia, New Zealand and South Africa.

Even having finally secured a place in an elite annual competition, the southern hemisphere's Rugby Championship, they still have to overcome the handicaps of an amateur rugby nation with a small pool of full-time professional players.

Yet it is that amateur ethos, grounded in a tight club system, that has earned the admiration of the world and has fired up the Pumas deep into the professional era, imbued by the values of a sport they strongly believe to be a model for life in any sphere.

The Pumas have had their ups and downs, golden periods and others when the odds were stacked against them through issues sometimes of their own making, like turning their backs on talents who left to play mainly in Europe lured by perks in the 1990s, when open professionalism was already just around the corner, and limited international competition.

After their brilliant third place at the 2007 World Cup in France, Argentina found a place in the Rugby Championship in 2012, thanks above all to the efforts of former captain Agustín Pichot. This helped them reach the World Cup semi-finals for the second time in England in 2015.

Ironically, though, the solution to Argentina's need for a nucleus of home-based professionals that had been resolved with their entry to Super Rugby as the Jaguares franchise in 2016 produced a new 'problem': a loaded calendar like never before for a squad of 40-odd players who doubled as the Pumas squad.

Playing at least 16 matches as Jaguares before donning the Pumas shirt for 12 Test matches a year took its toll. Being together all year like a club had some advantages but these were outweighed by the lack of minutes on the field for all but the first-choice squad and limited internal competition.

After reaching the Super Rugby final for the first time in their fourth season in 2019, the team had no proper break before the Rugby Championship and the continuity in the team that might have appeared ideal backfired at the World Cup in Japan.

Despite these difficulties, and going a year without playing a Test owing to the disruptions of the coronavirus pandemic, the Pumas managed some fine performances in the 2020 Tri-Nations Rugby Championship including a first win over New Zealand.

This boosted Argentina's confidence for the 2023 World Cup in France, where the Pumas hoped to equal or better their 2007 performance with a déjà vu feeling in the build-up.

As in 2007, there was a large number of Argentina internationals playing for European clubs after the Jaguares Super Rugby franchise was disbanded due to the Covid-19 pandemic, with the likelihood that the head coach would be relying on many exiles, quite the opposite of Japan 2019.

ONE

TRIES

ARGENTINA'S JOURNEY TO the higher reaches of rugby was marked by some iconic tries, starting with centre Marcelo Pascual's dramatic diving score to set the new Pumas on the way to their historic 11–6 victory over the Junior Springboks in Johannesburg in 1965.

Few sports photographs have been published as many times in Argentina as that of Pascual's leap over the line and almost certainly none of a rugby match, coming close to the picture of Diego Maradona's 'Hand of God' goal against England at football's 1986 World Cup.

It was the opening score of the Test in the 16th minute and was followed by further tries from wing Eduardo España, for a 6–0 half-time lead, and flanker Raúl Loyola, converted by fly-half Eduardo Poggi, to go 11–0 up early in the second half. The South Africans replied with two tries from scrum-half Kid du Preez.

'The South Africans really are our rugby godfathers; they opened the doors of international rugby to us,' said flanker Héctor 'Pochola' Silva, who at 20 was hailed on that tour as so good that had he been South African he would have been a Springbok for the quality of his all-round game.

Argentina really came to the notice of the major rugby countries when they almost beat Wales, the reigning Five Nations Grand Slam champions, in October 1976, a breakaway try by wing Jorge Gauweloose sparking a comeback from 17–6 down to almost snatch victory at Cardiff Arms Park.

'Then came the drama,' wrote Clem Thomas in his report for the *Observer*. 'Sansot, the brilliant young Argentine full back, came into the line to take a superb pass from Travaglini, and with a dazzling change of pace split the defence and put away Gauweloose, who went round JPR Williams and then cut in to score at the posts and Porta converted.'

The team included three players that Thomas, a former Wales flanker turned journalist and author, called world class in his report: Martín Sansot, centre Alejandro Travaglini and fly-half Hugo Porta.

Another try, followed by a penalty, both by centre Gonzalo Béccar Varela, put the Pumas 19–17 ahead in injury time.

But fly-half Phil Bennett rescued Wales with a penalty from the last kick of the match – given away by a dangerous tackle by Travaglini – and Wales won 20–19, defending an unbeaten home record dating back to their loss to New Zealand in 1972.

Two years later, another leap was how wing Marcelo Campo resolved matters in a split second as he faced a wall of players defending their line at Twickenham when Hugo Porta captained Argentina in their first meeting with England.

Taking a pass from Porta at speed, Campo leapt over the defenders to touch down and give the Pumas the lead in a 13–13 draw against what was termed an England XV.

An indication of just how much Argentina relied on place kicking in the days when they were playing catch-up with the most successful nations was fly-half Gonzalo Quesada becoming the top scorer of the 1999 World Cup with 102 points thanks to his accuracy with the boot.

The breakthrough Argentina had dreamt of since their failures at the first three World Cups came from the try scored by wing

Diego Albanese when the Pumas upset Ireland 28–24 in the French city of Lens to reach the quarter-finals for the first time.

Ireland's coach Warren Gatland believed his pack was better than Argentina's and would win the day. This thinking looked like being borne out as a kicking duel between Ireland fly-half David Humphreys and Quesada stood at 24–18 to the Irish with seven minutes remaining.

The Pumas had been behind throughout the match, 15–9 at half-time, 21–9 by the fourth minute of the second half, but they had worked their way back and with 12 minutes remaining they found new wind with a key change in the backs which worked to perfection for their coach, New Zealander Alex Wyllie.

Wyllie sent on a young Felipe Contepomi at fly-half with Quesada withdrawing to full back and Ignacio 'Nani' Corleto coming off. Five minutes later Albanese crossed the line after a scrum between halfway and the Irish 22.

'Albanese's try came from a move we practised often for when we might try to take the initiative,' captain Lisandro Arbizu said. 'And it was a lovely reward to be able to use it in that moment of such pressure.

'There is a decoy by the first centre (Arbizu himself) and then a second decoy with the ball bypassing the full back (Quesada at that stage) and reaching the wing.'

Quesada's conversion put Argentina in front for the first time in the match at 25–24 and his seventh penalty one minute from time gave the Pumas a four-point lead, leaving Ireland needing at least a try to save the match and meet France in a quarter-final at home in Dublin.

The Pumas kept the Irish at bay for a tantalising, seemingly eternal nine minutes, three more than the additional time announced after 80, before the final whistle went and they erupted with joy. 'Bloody nine minutes,' was Wyllie's reaction.

Nani Corleto's was the try that stunned France and most of the rugby world, sending the Pumas on their way to a huge 17–12 upset against the host nation in the opening match of the

2007 tournament.

Argentina dominated from the start and were 9–3 ahead on penalties when left wing Horacio Agulla intercepted a pass by flanker Rémy Martin and fed Manuel Contepomi whose pass found Corleto and the full back sped on a diagonal run across the Stade de France pitch to the far corner.

Further penalties from Felipe Contepomi and France fly-half David Skréla had the Pumas 17–9 up at the break and another Skréla penalty provided the only points of a second half in which the crowd were left stunned by Argentina's dominance of the reigning Six Nations champions.

Corleto, recalling the match for *La Nación* several years later, said: 'Our confidence was high and we knew that most of us had reached that moment with a lot of experience, accustomed to do-or-die situations.'

The full back also went on an attacking run down the left, sparking a cross-field move involving almost half the team and finished by Federico Martín Aramburú in the corner on the right when Argentina beat France again 34–10 in the bronze medal match at the Parc des Princes 42 days later, one of five tries on the shortlist for best of the year.

A match analysis in *La Nación*, every bit as impassioned as the Pumas' performance, described the team as 'an example of how to realise the most daring dreams and how far one can go if passion is the mobilising force'.

And looking to what lay ahead for the Pumas, it added: 'They have always had to justify their demands but now there can be no arguments against taking proper notice of them, the International Board (now World Rugby) to open doors for them and the UAR (Unión Argentina de Rugby) to not be so mean in their support.'

In New Zealand in 2011, Argentina trailed Scotland by six points in their key pool match when replacement wing Lucas González Amorosino took a pass from centre Marcelo Bosch and went on a run from the Scottish 22, weaving past five defenders for the late try converted by Felipe Contepomi that gave them a 13–12 win and a quarter-final berth for the third time in four World Cups.

Ireland were again the barrier to breach, this time for a place in the semi-finals, when the sides met at Cardiff's Millennium Stadium in a 2015 tournament marked by Argentina's more expansive game.

Tries scored by centre Matías Moroni and wing Juan Imhoff, from a perfectly weighted chip ahead by Santiago Cordero, in the opening ten minutes ensured Argentina were always ahead even though Ireland twice pulled back to within three points.

Imhoff went for a spectacular finish when he leapt for his second try under the posts to secure Argentina's place in the last four for the second time – a leap reminiscent of Pascual's half a century earlier.

Nicolás Sánchez's try against New Zealand in November 2020, chipping over the defence and touching down under the posts, was not the most spectacular but certainly one of Argentina's most significant as he inspired the Pumas to their first victory over the All Blacks.

The fly-half, who had been top scorer at the 2015 World Cup, put a disappointing 2019 tournament behind him by scoring all of Argentina's points in a 25–15 victory in the three-nation (in the absence of then world champions South Africa) Rugby Championship.

TWO

BIRTH

ARGENTINA'S FIRST RUGBY venture abroad was a landmark tour of southern Africa in 1965 that gave birth to the Pumas.

The two-month tour, including 16 matches – 11 wins, four defeats and one draw – forged the Pumas' spirit while cementing a rugby relationship with South Africa.

The highlight was Argentina's 16–11 victory over the Junior Springboks at Ellis Park in Johannesburg. It is recalled, along with an iconic photo of Marcelo Pascual's dive over the line for the opening try, whenever Argentina reach a new milestone in their rugby history.

South African reporters covering the tour debut match – a 17–12 defeat against Zimbabwe (still Rhodesia at the time) in Salisbury – asked about the animal that featured on their badge but found the name yaguareté, a jaguar from the north of Argentina, too difficult to pronounce.

'One of them said, "The yaguarewhat?" and as he couldn't pronounce it he said, "Well, puma,"' recalled Ricardo Handley, one of the hookers in the tour party, who played for the Old Georgian club in Buenos Aires.

The 'error' has been attributed separately to more than one South African journalist looking for a name for the team to stand alongside their own Springbok or Australia's Wallaby.

Another version had it that when newspapers reported on the team's first practice in Rhodesia, the article expressed surprise at the speed and agility of the Argentine players and compared them to pumas (poemas in Afrikaans), thinking that was the animal on their badges.

Never mind which was the true or first version, the name was a perfect fit, easier for English speakers to pronounce and write, and came to symbolise an Argentine international rugby player in the light blue and white striped colours, a player with the passion and spirit to overcome the greatest odds.

The Argentines were also told the animal on their crest was facing the wrong way, outwards, and should be pointing towards the heart of the wearer of a team shirt or blazer. Assistant coach Alberto Camardón said with some embarrassment, 'We'll have to change it.'

It is not clear exactly when the change was made. The animal is still facing outwards on the Pumas shirts in photos of their matches against the touring South African Gazelles in 1966, but had been turned inwards by the time of the first visit of Wales to Argentina in 1968.

After Argentina had joined the Rugby Championship nearly 50 years later, the UAR introduced a modernised badge at the close of the 2013 season with a sleeker-looking yaguareté pointing outwards again, as if looking for new horizons.

The late former South African Rugby Board chairman Danie Craven was the man responsible for Argentina's breakthrough in international rugby, inviting them to tour his country in 1965.

'Gato' (cat) Handley takes up the story: 'In 1964, Danie Craven, who as you know was known as Mr Rugby, came to watch the South American Championship in Brazil and said Argentina had lots of possibilities of improving their game and playing international rugby.

'He invited Argentina to tour South Africa in 1965 and he also sent one of his best trainers, Izak van Heerden, a month before the tour to train us in Buenos Aires and then be part of the coaching team during the tour which lasted two months.'

Van Heerden, who had a reputation as an innovative coach and tactician, put the Argentines through a far more demanding and at times painful fitness regime than they had ever experienced but he endeared himself to the players who soon found him a nickname, Tito.

'The day of the first training session, at Gimnasia y Esgrima, there was torrential rain. Those days, when the weather was bad we didn't do anything. Van Heerden arrived and saw there was nobody on the pitch. We were in the bar playing Truco (a popular Argentine card game),' recalls the team's captain, lock Aitor Otaño.

'The guy made us change at once. We did two infernal hours of training including frog jumps and crawling . . . He put us through a routine we were unaccustomed to – very tough. We did two shifts, morning and night, and in between we had our jobs.

'Every night when I got home, my wife would leave me a note by the door which said: "We're well, the kids are growing," . . . It was very hard but we saw the results.'

Handley adds: 'Something to remember was that not all the best players went to South Africa in 1965, because it was two months and many players had work or were studying. So the team that went had six or seven players with experience but most of us were 21, 22, 23-year-old boys.

'The first three or four matches were very tough. South Africans as you know are a tough group; they're very physical and they knocked the shit out of us in the first couple of games.

'We went to Rhodesia first and were unlucky to lose because our kicker had an off day.'

The Argentines had plenty of chances to win the match but place kicker Roberto 'Bobe' Cazenave, their full back, missed a string of penalties. He was wearing a new pair of boots for the first time and could not get comfortable in them.

So Argentina, despite scoring four tries at a time when these were only worth three points, the same as penalties, lost 17–12.

'Then we lost the next game in South Africa and decided we weren't going to take it any more and we toughened up and met them with the same kind of game as we were receiving.

'From then on we were successful and won most of our matches, and there were tough matches against country districts who were farmers and miners – tough individuals. So it really was the start of Argentina beginning to have an international team.'

South Africa, who had previously sent touring Junior Springboks teams to Argentina in 1932 and 1959, sought ever more keenly to keep alive rugby links with other countries after their government's apartheid policy of racial segregation, instituted in 1948, earned the opprobrium of most of the world.

Craven foresaw the Springboks, the sports team most identified with Afrikaner supremacy, being ostracised more and more and that their isolation would have a detrimental effect on the team, and his fears were reinforced with the country's ban from the 1964 Tokyo Olympic Games.

At the time the Argentines were in South Africa in 1965, the Springboks were on a tour of Australia and New Zealand and they lost the first Test against the Wallabies earlier on the day of the Pumas' victory over the Junior Springboks, the biggest match thus far in Argentina's rugby history.

The Springboks lost to Australia again in the second Test in Brisbane on the last day of Argentina's tour, a worrying development for Craven back home, and they would go on to lose the series in New Zealand 3–1.

Van Heerden was not a fan of the Springboks' style of play based on forward power and defence and was not disappointed when the Argentines he accompanied throughout their tour showed a balanced game of good scrummaging and skills running with the ball, winning friends in the white crowds and enjoying support from the segregated black population.

Fly-half Eduardo Poggi's place kicking, coming round to the ball from the side and hitting it with the inside of his instep, caused initial hilarity among South Africans, who had only seen kickers hit it straight with the toe of their boots, before being admired for its effectiveness.

When the Pumas resoundingly beat Southern Universities 22–6 at Newlands in Cape Town in the 11th match of the tour, they were feted with the headline 'The Pumas destroy the cradle of South African rugby' in the *Cape Times*.

'Argentine Springbok'

THE ARGENTINE PLAYER who stood out for South Africans was back-row forward Silva, fondly known as 'the man with the headband', many saying he had all the attributes of a Springbok.

Silva, then 20, was an all-rounder who had begun his playing career with Los Tilos, a small, second division club in the city of La Plata, at full back.

He had to have been very good to get noticed in a rugby backwater and his rampaging style was best suited to the back row where he had all his games for Argentina and impressed the great Hugo Porta, who said of him: 'He is the ideal image of a Puma, the player we all at some time wished to be.'

In 1966, Silva was part of the team that lost a home series 2–0 to the Gazelles, the Springboks' under-23 team who were then coached by Van Heerden, before captaining his country when they returned to South Africa in 1971 and shared a two-match series 1–1 with the Gazelles.

Handley, another who returned to South Africa on the 1971 tour, said: 'Most of us young guys who went on the 1965 tour became a very competitive team over the next five or six years – we beat Wales, Ireland, Scotland and the South African Gazelles. We grew tremendously in the 1970s.

'Most of the players in that [Gazelles] team became Springboks so Argentina took a very big leap and we have to be very grateful to South Africa because, as we always say, they were our godfathers; they launched us into the international field of rugby.'

Argentina had held their internationals at the 12,000-capacity stadium of Gimnasia y Esgrima (Gymnastics and Fencing), a traditional club in the Palermo district of Buenos Aires and commonly known as GEBA.

In the search to accommodate more fans, the Pumas moved to Club Atlético Ferro Carril Oeste (western railway), which holds twice the number of spectators, in 1970 for the visit of Ireland. Ferro was another multi-sports club with a football team that won two national league titles in the early 1980s and a basketball team.

Fans were becoming more demanding with each Argentine exploit and fully expected a victory over the Gazelles after they had been held 13–13 by the Buenos Aires champions San Isidro Club (SIC) in their opening match of a tour of Argentina in 1972.

The Gazelles, stung by a 12–0 defeat in Pretoria the previous year in the shared series with the Pumas, were too strong in the first meeting and won 14–6, but the Argentines hit back with an 18–16 victory in the second.

However, Silva, who also regarded South Africa as 'almost our spiritual godfathers', was not involved in that 1972 series.

He was left in the cold by the Argentine union that year because he had appeared in an advertising spot for a liniment, contravening its strict amateur rules. He wrote in his autobiography *Pochola Silva, Pasión y Coraje* (passion and courage) that such a decision would be laughable at the time the book was published in 2001.

The sanction was indefinite and tore Silva from the Pumas in his prime and when he was captain. It took seven years and the support of coach Angel 'Papuchi' Guastella before he was able to make a Pumas comeback and write another chapter in his rich playing career.

After some intense training on his own which included long sessions carrying his little son up and down the stairs at home, he came into a team mostly made up of a new generation preparing to face England at Twickenham in 1978.

Many of the players who had almost beaten Wales in Cardiff in 1976, going down 20–19 to a Phil Bennett penalty in injury time, were eligible for the tour but ran foul of the UAR Council over their choice of captain, centre Arturo Rodríguez Jurado, who had done an advertising spot for rugby boots.

Neither side budged in the stand-off, the coaches resigned and ten players followed their lead, refusing to take part in the 1977 South American Championship and were suspended from the national team, so it was Porta who led them on the 1978 tour.

Fans at home had not been too pleased with recent performances and Silva recalled vividly one shouting at some of the Pumas during a National Provincial Championship match in Rosario: 'Hey, when you cross the English Channel, all of you can jump in.'

Nicknamed 'Uncle' by the younger players and known to steady their nerves by saying, 'Relax, you're playing with Dad', Silva was 34 when Argentina drew 13–13 with England. He also went on tour with the Pumas to New Zealand and played in a shared series with Australia in Buenos Aires in 1979.

South Africa found a way to keep competing during the international boycott by inviting a South America XV, effectively the Pumas in disguise, to play series at home and away in the early 1980s. Silva played in one of the matches in 1980, then bowed out against the Rest of the World.

The Argentine government had joined the boycott of South Africa and refused the UAR permission to send the Pumas to play the Springboks so players and coaches got around the issue by touring as the South American Jaguars.

Silva went on to coach the Pumas at the first World Cup in New Zealand in 1987 which was a disappointment after an opening defeat by Fiji, who took the quarter-final slot that Argentina had been seeded for. The Pumas beat Italy and lost to the All Blacks.

The South American team, featuring a full Argentina side, managed one notable 21–12 victory in Bloemfontein in 1982 with a brilliant performance by Porta, who scored all their points with a 'poker': try, conversion, drop goal and four penalties.

Argentina had its own serious political problems with the military regime's genocidal 'Dirty War' against dissidents and its ill-fated invasion of the British-held Falkland Islands in the South Atlantic on 2 April 1982, the day before that momentous victory for the Jaguars which received scant attention back home at the time.

Porta, whose close relationship with South Africa included his appointment as ambassador to Pretoria by President Carlos Menem in 1991 when the countries reopened diplomatic relations after the release from prison of Nelson Mandela, was carried off on the shoulders of South African fans after the win.

Also in the victorious team was flanker Jorge Allen, who afterwards played for Natal for two seasons, the first Argentine to play for a South African team. At the time he had one Pumas cap, against Canada in 1981, and did not win his second until 1985 when he was back at CASI (Club Atlético San Isidro) and part of the side that beat France and drew with New Zealand before succeeding Porta as captain in 1988.

The match in Bloemfontein in 1982 was an unofficial first Test win over the Springboks before Argentina and South Africa had even met at official international level. It would take 11 years for their first Test meeting and 33 years for the Pumas to break their duck after two near misses.

South Africa won the first Test 29–26 on their first tour of Argentina in 1993 and the second Test 52–23. In the next two series in 1994 and 1996 South Africa scored at least 40 points and won by at least 20 in all four Tests.

When the Springboks were upset 28–27 by Buenos Aires on the 1993 tour, centre Marcelo Loffreda became the first Argentine player to beat South Africa twice, having also taken part in the 1982 Bloemfontein Test win for the Jaguars.

Loffreda played for the Pumas for the last time as captain on the 1994 tour, during which he scored a memorable try in the first Test at Port Elizabeth.

The second Test in Johannesburg was marked by the debut of young fly-half José Cilley, grandson of Jorge Cilley who played for Argentina in the 1930s.

Argentina found themselves without a fly-half due to injuries during the week prior to the Test at Ellis Park and made an emergency call to Buenos Aires for a replacement.

Cilley landed at Johannesburg airport three hours before kick-off after the long flight from Argentina and was driven straight to Ellis Park where he made a mockery of the norms of preparation for a top-level competition, scoring 21 points including a try in a 46–26 defeat. Cilley would go on to play at the 1995 World Cup and win 16 caps.

With Loffreda as Argentina's coach, South Africa were hard pressed to win 37–33 when the sides met at the River Plate stadium in 2000 and 26–25 at Port Elizabeth in 2003.

After South Africa's 2007 World Cup semi-final win over Argentina, the Springboks won the first match of the newly constituted Rugby Championship 27–6 in 2012 but the Pumas marked their home debut a week later with a 16–16 draw against the same opponents in Mendoza.

The Pumas enjoyed their first victory against South Africa in 2015, 37–25 fittingly in a Rugby Championship match in Durban that doubled as a 50th anniversary celebration of Argentina's 1965 tour.

There were a dozen veterans of that landmark tour in the stands that day, including Handley, Silva and two other former Pumas coaches, Luis Gradín and José Luis Imhoff, whose son Juan scored a hat-trick of tries.

South Africa won their World Cup semi-final in London less than three months later and the Pumas got their first home victory, 26–24 in Salta the following year.

Loffreda, who played in four Tests for the Jaguars, said the

Argentina players thought it was natural to separate politics from sport and had no objection to playing for a combined team like the South America XV in South Africa during the apartheid era.

'I was quite young and it was like saying, "OK, I don't want to know about politics, all I want to do is play." At that time there probably wasn't much notice taken of a disguised Argentina team going to South Africa for sporting reasons. I didn't think it could be so serious.

'Looking at it now from a different perspective, and a lot older, I think it was maybe not right to go, given the situation. Also now there is much greater awareness and care in everything to do with discrimination and separation. I now think it wasn't a good decision from a social, human and political perspective.'

In 2011, Loffreda joined the non-profit humanitarian organisation Rugby sin Fronteras (rugby without borders), who have Nelson Mandela as one of their inspirations, on a trip to Robben Island to visit the prison where the South African leader, who died two years later, spent 18 of his 27 years' imprisonment by his country's apartheid regime.

THREE

AMATEUR SPIRIT

ARGENTINA HAVE A deeply entrenched amateur ethos in their game. They believe strongly in the amateur club system that feeds their national teams and would not like it tarnished by professionalism – even though their senior representative teams have now been fully professional since Argentina entered a team in Super Rugby in 2016.

The essence of those clubs is passing down the amateur spirit – rugby as a game to forge friendships, character and the joy of playing – from one generation to the next.

Families were part of the tapestry of a tight middle-class community at the core of this once minority sport in a country where football is king and the bilingual Anglo-Argentine schools played a role in the development of the game.

The Old Georgian club that won successive first division titles from 1937 to 1939 was formed by old boys of St George's College, a school modelled on English public schools, in the southern Buenos Aires suburb of Quilmes.

Rugby in Argentina became organised with the foundation in 1899 of the River Plate Rugby Union Championship, predecessor of the Unión Argentina de Rugby (UAR).

Of the five founding clubs, four remain in existence: Belgrano Athletic, Lomas Athletic, Rosario Athletic, now Atlético del Rosario, and Buenos Aires FC, which through a merger of two clubs in 1951 became Buenos Aires Cricket and Rugby Club, commonly known as Biei (beeay: using phonetic Spanish spelling for BA).

Athletic was the common denominator of most of the earliest sports clubs in Argentina because it took some years to establish which game they were playing when even back in the 'home country' the divisions between the rules of football and rugby were only beginning to be firmly established.

Arturo Rodríguez Jurado, a powerful centre in the 1965 team 'christened' Pumas in South Africa who also won a series against the touring Wales XV in 1968, was the son of a former Argentina captain who was the winner of an Olympic boxing gold medal at the 1928 Games in Amsterdam.

The three Morgan brothers, Dudley, Miguel and Eduardo, nicknamed 'Winnie', preceded New Zealand's Barrett brothers by all playing together for Argentina in the match against Northern Universities on the Pumas' 1971 tour of South Africa, though not in a Test.

Winnie Morgan was a versatile, very quick back who played for Old Georgian and won ten caps on the wing between 1972 and 1973, then two more as captain and scrum-half partnering Hugo Porta on Argentina's first tour of France in 1975.

Playing on the wing, he set the Argentine individual points record in a single match with 50 (six tries and 13 conversions) in a 97–3 win against Paraguay in a South American Championship match in Sao Paulo in 1973. He also scored 31 in a 55–0 victory over Uruguay in the same week.

Paraguay were again on the receiving end when wing José Núñez Piossek set the try record of nine, 45 points, in a 144–0 rout in Montevideo in 2003.

Such statistics against weak South American opposition are, however, less significant than the points record against a major rugby country held by Felipe Contepomi, 31 including two tries playing at fly-half in a 41–31 home win against France in 2010, while wing José Luna also scored 31 against Romania in 1996.

Former Pumas captain and later World Rugby vice-president Agustín Pichot's family is strongly associated with Club Atlético San Isidro (CASI), as are the Allens and Travaglinis.

Jorge 'Georgy' Allen was a flanker in the great side of the 1980s and later captained the Pumas. His father Leslie played in the 1951 South American Championship and his two brothers Gabriel, a former CASI president, and Matías also represented their country.

Leslie Allen was born in Rosario where his father was one of hundreds of Britons contracted to work on the railways, many of whom played a part in the foundation of sports clubs in Argentina.

When he moved to Buenos Aires as a young man, Leslie Allen joined CASI. To this day there is a strong link between his first club Atlético del Rosario, founded in 1867 originally as a cricket club, and CASI, with members of one automatically being 'socios' of the other.

Noted particularly for their tackling, Leslie and his three sons all won club titles with CASI. Georgy worked in South Africa and played for Natal before winning 29 caps in the back row and being named captain when Porta retired for the first time in 1987.

Alejandro Travaglini was a centre in the Pumas side of the 1970s that came within a whisker of beating Wales in Cardiff in 1976, and his nephew Gabriel played in the back row of the team captained by Hugo Porta, winning 23 caps including his final three at the 1987 World Cup.

The big Iachetti brothers, Alejandro and Marcos, lined up in the second row against Australia in a shared two-match series in 1979, while the scrum-half was Ricardo Landajo, whose son Martín played for the Pumas at the 2015 World Cup – also at number nine.

Two pairs of brothers were in the side that beat France for the first time in 1985. The Lanza twins Juan and Pedro were the wings and Javier and Bernardo Miguens played at scrum-half and full back respectively. A third Miguens brother Hugo also played for Argentina and captained them in 1973.

Tomás Cubelli, for some years Martín Landajo's rival for the Pumas number nine jersey, is the son of hooker Alejandro Cubelli, a member of one of many top-notch front rows with Fernando Morel and Diego Cash.

Nicolás Fernández Miranda, Pichot's main rival as Pumas scrum-half for more than a decade, and his brother Juan played for the most successful club in the Buenos Aires first division this century, Hindú.

The Contepomi family's involvement in rugby runs deep, as does their relationship with the Villegas family.

Carlos Contepomi's twin sons Manuel and Felipe, Argentina's second highest points scorer in international matches with 651 between 1998 and 2013, were the centres in the 2007 World Cup bronze medal team.

Carlos, capped twice as a fly-half in 1964 and known to all his friends as 'Pomi', was manager of the 1976 side that toured Wales and England and was coached by Carlos 'Veco' Villegas.

Nearly 30 years later, Pomi was back in Cardiff to watch his son Felipe captain Argentina when they gave the British and Irish Lions a warm-up – and a fright in an unexpected 25–25 draw – at the Millennium (now Principality) Stadium ahead of their 2005 tour of New Zealand.

That night in Cardiff also served to renew friendships between Argentine and Welsh rugby men, forged during the 1970s.

'How could I not come to Cardiff to see my son play against the Lions and captain the Pumas,' Pomi told me on the eve of the match before disappearing into the streets of Cardiff with several Welsh friends for a night on the town.

Tragedy

POMI AND VECO forged a friendship when Contepomi was put in charge of Argentina's national teams commission and Villegas was Pumas coach, but that would be cut short tragically in June 1988 when Veco, who was 43, and his wife were killed in a plane crash.

Pomi tells a story that on the eve of Veco's death the pair went to the Vélez Sarsfield stadium where they watched the touring France side featuring the likes of Serge Blanco, Philippe Sella and Pierre Berbizier thump Buenos Aires 82–0.

'Afterwards, we went to the changing room to see the Buenos Aires players, who were very down, and told them there is always a second chance; don't let this defeat embitter you – you'll soon get revenge.

'But we were also depressed and decided not to go to the post-match dinner to which we were invited: "It's going to be a cemetery," Veco said.'

So the pair ate takeaway pizza at Veco's house instead, and chatted into the early hours about family life in general and their respective children's education and future – with the eldest of Contepomi's seven close to finishing school – never even imagining the tragedy that would unfold the following day.

Pomi was stunned when he learnt the next morning that the plane taking Veco and his wife to the north-eastern city of Posadas had crashed killing everyone on board.

He helped the Villegas family overcome this huge loss and make plans for the four orphaned children, aged between one and 11, to live with their grandmother.

Having developed a strong bond, incorporating them into the Contepomis' lives at weekends and taking them on holiday, Pomi took the four into his home when their grandmother died nine years later, taking advantage of the rooms vacated by his three eldest who had left, one as a priest, the others having married.

'It helped a lot for their development because it was very hard for them and that assimilation means that today I can say that instead of 25 grandchildren I have 32.'

Pomi said he was repaid when the distractions of so much family activity in a crowded home, birthday parties, friends coming round, helped him to cope when his wife suffered from Alzheimer's.

Strong rivalries also produced schisms within the governing body and even clubs.

The Buenos Aires northern suburb of San Isidro is at the heart of Argentine rugby and called its capital.

In 1934, as a result of an incident among the players after a match in which CASI were at home to title rivals Gimnasia y Esgrima, the home team's authorities handed down a suspension to most of their club's first team.

Many players did not accept this decision and left, founding a new club, SIC (San Isidro Club), a few kilometres down the road.

The two clubs have been bitter rivals ever since and their derby is the big 'clásico' of the Buenos Aires first division championship.

Up to SIC's 2019 championship victory, between them they had won 59 titles: CASI 33 and SIC 26.

The amateur spirit that drove Argentina to their early achievements against the odds would not have been possible without the immense character of their leading players. It is also this spirit that has seen the team emerge even stronger from many setbacks.

Schisms between the UAR and players, confrontations among players themselves, conflicts with coaches, many of them over the perceived dangers of professionalism, all produced rifts that sometimes had detrimental effects on the team but were also just as likely to spawn a new team and drive them to greater deeds.

One such schism fell between the near miss in the 20–19 defeat against Wales at Cardiff Arms Park in 1976 and the 13–13 draw with the English at Twickenham two years later.

Eliseo 'Chapa' Branca, one of Argentina's best ever locks who made his Test debut at 19 in the 1976 match in Cardiff and bowed out in a win and shared series at home to England in 1990, explains what happened:

'In 1977, coaches Veco Villegas and Emilio Perasso resigned when the UAR rejected their choice of Arturo Rodríguez Jurado as captain of the team they were preparing for the South American Championship.

'The union didn't want him [as captain] because he had made an advertisement for boots and he appeared like James Bond on TV, not dressed as a rugby player, mind you,' Branca said.

Ten players supported the coaches, refusing to join the squad, and were duly suspended. The president of Branca's club Curupaytí was on the UAR board that handed down the suspension so he left to join CASI.

'We were naive; it was a political problem. Arturo wasn't suspended, the only thing the UAR said was he couldn't be captain.

'The coaches should have said: "Lads, you play and don't make an issue of it." But they said, "You decide what you're going to do; we're resigning," and that was a blow so we supported them in good faith.

'We were suspended for five years but I didn't even have a contract. Part of the flag of amateur rugby is that I play when I feel like it.'

A new team with some veterans, but a raft of young players who would soon make a name for themselves as Pumas, was led by Hugo Porta, fast emerging as one of the world's best fly-halves, in their landmark 13–13 draw with an England XV at Twickenham in 1978.

Less than two years later the suspension, which also affected scrum-half Daniel Baetti, was lifted and he and Branca were back in the Pumas side for a home series against Fiji.

There were controversial selection decisions and changes of coaching staff that undermined Argentine World Cup campaigns and dashed the Pumas' hopes of progressing beyond the pool phase in 1987, 1991 and 1995.

This was a source of huge disappointment after the Pumas had proved with victories or fine performances in defeat that they could compete as equals with the established leading nations in the game.

1965 legacy

BRANCA BELIEVES THE Pumas of the mid-1980s were as good as the team that won the bronze medal at the 2007 World Cup. 'When I made my debut in 1976 we had very good three-quarters but lacked some mobility and size in the forwards.

'But from my generation there was an influx of big forwards who could play. If it hadn't been for that suspension [in 1977], two generations could have come together to make a superb team but there was always a problem in the middle.

'Then in 1985, with a new group of backs, we beat France. That's when there was a boom in the Pumas' popularity and the appearance of merchandising. Lots of brands approached the Pumas bringing in funds and there was more emphasis on preparing the team physically.'

Many days training and playing in the South American Championship before New Zealand toured Argentina later that year helped to seal another big result.

The Pumas held the All Blacks to a 21–21 draw in the second Test, a result that stood as their best for 35 years against New Zealand until they broke the jinx in the 2020 Rugby Championship.

'The team was as good as, if not better than, that of 2007,' Branca said. 'We won all the matches we had to win and that's why the 2007 team appeared . . . That's down to us and we have a debt with the 1965 Pumas.

'If [Argentina] hadn't beaten the Junior Springboks in 1965, I wouldn't have played rugby, maybe another sport. It's all linked. I don't think in any way that the 2007 team was better than ours.'

Although the players remained 100 per cent amateur, the UAR began to accept and benefit from advertising in the mid-1980s.

'When I started out, I wasn't allowed to wear the little badge of the brand that gave me my [playing] clothes. I'd be told to "cover it",' said Branca, who turned down offers to play abroad because he would have been banned from all rugby at home including the Pumas.

'But I didn't see it as a bad thing to have good training, good physical coaching, to feed the playing side with that money – not get paid to play but yes to travel. There were lots of extremists [against that] whose ideals badly affected our competitiveness.

'After the '80s there was a big slump until we found the route that Pichot found. The first step was the first World Cup, the total flop of amateurism – the other teams were prepared differently.

'And when we got beaten by almost 100 points by New Zealand [in 1997] that's when Gradín, who was the president of the UAR, realised that could not go on.'

Luis 'Lucho' Gradín, a member of the original Pumas who toured southern Africa in 1965 (who later became the team's coach and eventually UAR president in 1996), explains the special character of Argentine rugby.

'A very important consideration is the nature of our clubs. We have a club structure that is British but with a Latin content, which gives you a very particular establishment.

'This produced difficulties in the running of the unions that are meant to govern the game, facing constant clashes of interests with people pulling in opposite directions.

'But we gradually found our way and managed a necessary balance between clubs, provincial unions and the Argentine union so that today we have that balance, though we are forever wary of breaking it.'

Gradín opened the doors to the previously banned professional exiles with front-row forward Federico Méndez the first welcomed back into the fold.

The game in Argentina was centred in Buenos Aires virtually up to the change of the millennium, with its club championships run by the UAR. But in 1995, Buenos Aires and the UAR split, leaving the national entity to look after federal issues and the Pumas, while a new body, Unión de Rugby de Buenos Aires (URBA), took charge of domestic competitions in Buenos Aires province.

This split helped open UAR doors to directors, coaches and players from the country's other leading provincial unions which had had only marginal influence previously.

It tended to be rare for players from Rosario, Córdoba, Tucumán or Mendoza to be selected for the Pumas but at the 2019 World Cup in Japan, for the first time the squad had a minority of players who had learnt their rugby at clubs in the URBA.

The advent of professionalism, clandestine in the build-up to it becoming open in 1995, jarred with Argentina's determination to remain amateur and sometimes left the Pumas badly weakened in the face of much better-prepared teams.

It became inevitable that players would defect, especially in the case of Diego Domínguez, who forged a brilliant career with Italy after finding his path to the Pumas blocked by coaches reluctant to groom him as Porta's natural successor.

It did not help his cause that he was from Córdoba, not Buenos Aires. He went on tours of France in 1988 and New Zealand in 1989 but was only picked for a couple of midweek games. His only caps came in two South American Championship Tests but he went on to be capped by Italy more than 70 times.

The UAR outlawed such players, who were lured to the Italian championship by clubs providing good living conditions and perks though their primary motivation was to forge a rugby career.

Others who followed Domínguez included brilliant scrum-half Fabio 'Aguja' Gómez, who had shared a fine half-back partnership with Porta at their club Banco Nación, centre Fabián Turnes and veteran forwards Gustavo Milano and Serafín Dengra, who also had a spell in Australia.

In the early years of professional rugby, the gulf grew in the finance and support enjoyed by the leading nations and a small one like Argentina with meagre backing from the UAR, in addition to their lack of an annual major competition that limited their matches and time together in a season.

'The difference became much greater, definitely, in 1995, especially the physical compared with the European teams and even more so those of the southern hemisphere,' said Lisandro Arbizu, who became Argentina's youngest captain at 21 in 1992 and led the team in 48 of his 86 Tests in 11 years.

'However much commitment and dedication we had, we felt we were dropping further and further behind them. It was only after many of us started playing abroad that several things changed for the 1999 World Cup.'

The first professional given the green light to play for the Pumas was hooker Federico Méndez, who was then on the books of Natal, for the November 1996 home series against South Africa. He was followed by prop Mauricio Reggiardo of Castres for the tour of England the following month.

In 1999, New Zealander Alex Wyllie, a former All Blacks player and trainer who was being paid as a consultant, was left in sole charge after coach Héctor Méndez resigned and he steered the team to their first quarter-final at the World Cup weeks later.

One of the best number 8s Argentina has ever produced, Pablo Camerlinckx refused to become professional, turning down chances to play in France in the 1990s so as to retain his opportunities of being picked by the Pumas.

Yet he suffered a huge disappointment when, having been included by one coach in the squad for the 1999 World Cup, that coach was relieved of his post a few weeks before the tournament and his successor dropped three players including Camerlinckx in favour of his own choices.

FOUR

PUMAS PLUS

'At that time, if you went off to play professional rugby,
you became little more than a pariah in Argentina.'
Pablo Camerlinckx

THE DREAM OF most Argentine rugby players is to play for
the Pumas but there was a time when anyone good enough to do
so who went abroad to better himself by playing professionally
was banned from all rugby at home.

Pablo Camerlinckx, one of the best number 8s in Argentina in
the 1990s, had offers from various foreign clubs to join them in
the days of under-the-table professionalism, even after 1995 but
before Argentina belatedly lifted its ban.

For him, the all-important thing was playing for the Pumas
and he was like the majority of top players in the country in
turning down offers to turn professional.

Serge Blanco approached him to join Biarritz, at the time one
of Europe's top clubs, and he also could have gone to South
Africa, New Zealand, Australia or Ireland.

'I had offers to move over to professional rugby from 1989

when I went to the World Junior Championship (then under-19, organised by FIRA, won by Argentina) in Portugal. But at that time, if you went off to play professional rugby, you became little more than a pariah in Argentina, and you couldn't play any more in the Pumas or your club.

'It went open in 1995 so anywhere you went in 1989 was illegal and you got punished for that in Argentina; you couldn't play rugby any more.

'In any case, for me there was never any doubt that I played rugby for fun and as a way of making friends, and I had the grace of God to play for the Pumas for which I'm very proud and to become the best in my position for a long time. I never wanted to play rugby professionally.'

Camerlinckx, however, sees Argentina's progress into the professional ranks as a good and inevitable thing and essential now for players who still dream of wearing the Pumas colours.

'For me rugby is the club, my friends and no money can pay for that, but today I wouldn't see any other path [than the professional one] because if not I wouldn't be able to play for the national team and today it's a way of life, a career that can set you up for life.

'I have no doubt the change was well done. We had to go that way and what Agustín Pichot did was brilliant. I don't mind [the amateur clubs] being a feeding ground for the small percentage of players good enough to be professional.

'In Argentina it's all amateur. It's crazy what's happening – 400 amateur clubs feeding a few professional teams free, in exchange for nothing. The passion for rugby in Argentina is crazy, hard to explain and it needs analysing. My brother Enrique says professional rugby in Argentina is a business model to study at Harvard or some other university.'

And the amateur ethos is that 'something extra' that the Pumas have always had.

Camerlinckx said the 1990s were tough, a transition period for Argentina during which they lost 93–8 to the All Blacks on a tour of New Zealand, their worst ever result.

'I played in that match. It was humiliating but we played against super professionals and I got up every day to go to work, I trained at my club when I could and there I was playing against Zinzan Brooke; it was a terrible handicap and despite that we beat England and Australia [that year].

'I don't think it will ever change because Argentina is a third world country with people who think they are of the first world and the economy will never make it possible for the amateur clubs to turn professional.

'The people who play rugby in Argentina have a high standard of education – they're guys who have studied, who work, they have a different head – and those who get to professional rugby from the number of players in Argentina is 1 or 2 per cent. It's very difficult to make a go of living from rugby in Argentina.

'But it's why Argentine players have always been sought after – players born in the cradle of amateurism who give that little extra without expecting anything in return; that's what rugby here teaches you and that serves you well in life too.'

Camerlinckx's rugby career had its ups and downs. His strong character often got him into arguments with coaches and that sometimes led to him being dropped or overlooked for tours and even a World Cup.

'When I made my debut at 18 I had a big fight with coach Rodolfo "Michingo" O'Reilly and Raúl Sanz. I was promoted from the junior team, I was the captain and the rugby they played was all hitting, trying to get the upper hand by being macho, which I didn't share. I had to adapt or I wouldn't get a game.'

Between 1990 and 1996 he only played intermittently for the Pumas but after a longer run in the team he looked sure to be a part of the squad that made the Pumas' breakthrough at the 1999 World Cup where they reached the quarter-finals for the first time.

Instead he was one of three players dropped from the initial squad after a change of coach a few weeks before the tournament.

As it happened that coach went too, after two warm-up Tests on tour, resigning over differences with UAR officials and players. As captain Lisandro Arbizu put it, 'We were orphaned,' until New Zealander Alex Wyllie took charge on the cusp of the tournament.

FIVE

SAN ISIDRO

ARGENTINE SCRUMS EARNED the respect of their international rivals from the 1960s with club and provincial teams giving touring Test sides tough games and running up a series of impressive results.

Argentine beef became a popular term in English-speaking rugby circles when referring to forwards from the Pampas and the best Argentine front-row forwards became highly prized assets.

The two top clubs in San Isidro, the Buenos Aires suburb where the famous '*bajadita*' method of an almost horizontal shove was perfected, had a big influence on the Pumas of the 1970s and '80s.

The man responsible for the success of the *bajadita* was Veco Villegas, who carried his coaching methods to the Pumas once he had made his name as a coach at San Isidro Club (SIC).

Veco drew his ideas from Francisco 'Catamarca' Ocampo, who was impressed by the sheer superiority of the British team that toured Argentina in 1927, when he was 25.

Ocampo studied the game in depth in a bid to bring the Argentines closer to that ideal, avidly reading books and articles in English with the help of a dictionary.

He focused primarily on the scrum, arguing that everything else in the game flowed from that distinctive formation, and so developed ideas on a coordinated shove which became his legacy to Argentine rugby.

Villegas coached from the age of 25 until his untimely death at 43 in the plane crash, cementing that legacy as he carried through the ideals inherited from Ocampo at SIC, whom he coached to four consecutive Buenos Aires club championship titles in the early 1970s.

'I can't say if I was his successor because he had hundreds of disciples,' the modest Villegas said of Ocampo. 'But I did have a big advantage over him. I had him [as mentor] whereas he had no one.'

The key was *la bajadita* – from *bajar*, to go down. The scrum binds very low and all eight forwards push in unison to move the opposing pack off the ball.

Veco wasn't primarily looking to win the ball but the scrum, imposing supremacy. If his forwards also won the ball so much the better.

SIC and arch-rivals Club Atlético San Isidro (CASI) dominated the Buenos Aires club championship in the 1970s and '80s – one or the other won it between 1970 and 1988.

This was a period when the Pumas were trying to cement a place among the top rugby nations.

Papuchi Guastella, who had been the Pumas coach since their landmark tour of South Africa in 1965, was replaced after a disappointing tour of Ireland and Scotland in 1973 where two generations of players failed to gel and both Test matches were lost, having beaten both nations at home in the late 1960s.

Adverse weather conditions were particularly difficult for the Pumas in Ireland where the home team were bent on avenging a 2–0 series defeat in Argentina in 1970 and won the Test 21–8.

Argentina could have won the Test at Murrayfield at the end of the eight-match tour after tries by Hugo Porta and Alejandro

Travaglini but a drop goal by Colin Telfer snatched a 12–11 victory for Scotland.

Villegas and his SIC assistant Emilio 'Gringo' Perasso were then handed the job and picked a squad that included 16 players from their club, the reigning champions, for the 1974 visit of the French, naming ten in the team.

The Pumas played well and the Tests were close with losing margins of five and four points, but not everyone was happy with the predominance of a scrummaging and kicking game. Most of Argentina's points came from the boot of Hugo Porta whereas France won the overall try count 7–2.

The pressure brought to bear by those opposed to the SIC method welcomed CASI's title later in the year. A new UAR leadership dispensed with Veco and appointed two 1965 veterans, Eduardo Scharenberg and Eduardo Poggi, for the tour to France in 1975.

Porta complained that constant changes in coaches, which would continue to the turn of the century, prevented the team from building a strong base.

Former lock José Javier 'Tito' Fernández, who became a top coach with ten-time URBA champions Hindú, said: 'The undoubted influence exerted by SIC's successes sparked talk of two opposed currents in Argentine rugby. This schism did us a lot of harm.'

The new coaches cleaned out most of the SIC players, which may have been more of a political decision, but results on Argentina's first visit to France, where they were unprepared for stern opposition from regional sides, were poor and Veco was brought back in.

Given this new chance, Veco did not call up a mass of SIC players again but instead went for all the best players regardless of which clubs they played for. Several had emerged on the French tour like brilliant full back Martín Sansot who would impress Welsh crowds on tour in Wales.

Cardiff 1976

THE 1976 TOUR was a great success and Argentina were one penalty away from achieving a bombshell of a result in their 20–19 defeat by Wales, then the Five Nations Grand Slam champions.

Argentina's team manager Carlos Contepomi recalled a group of South African rugby directors sitting behind him at Cardiff Arms Park and one of them saying to him: 'You don't know the significance of this revolution for the world, that a team should come from a country that is not among the top rugby nations and almost beat the best team in Europe at the time.'

The Argentines had felt confident going into the big test of a highly successful and enjoyable tour.

Veco told his players afterwards that the Wales team manager had been impressed by their attitude during the national anthems, the ritual of holding each other firmly in line.

With the Pumas leading by two points in injury time, tall centre Alejandro Travaglini was caught wrong-footed by JPR Williams as the full back launched a last gasp counter-attack and stuck out his arm in an instinctive action to try to stop him, catching him almost at throat height.

Phil Bennett kicked the penalty but the Argentines had given Wales a mighty scare running in two fine tries through Jorge Gauweloose and Daniel Béccar Varela after falling 17–6 behind early in the second half to tries by Gareth Edwards and Gerald Davies.

Fullback Martín Sansot told me that a cheeky move by Bennett gained him the advantage of taking the kick from several metres closer to the posts than the actual place of the incident. 'The funniest thing was Phil Bennett's very Latin attitude, chasing the referee, Norman Sanson of Scotland, who, when he turned round after admonishing Travaglini for his dangerous action, Phil was right behind him some eight to ten steps closer to our in-goal.

'I kept that ball which Phil kicked. It barely got over the bar. I reckon he would never have converted that kick from the spot of the original infringement.'

The papers said Wales winners on points, Argentina moral winners. Pity.

Fly-half Hugo Porta told a British newspaper reporter that he should take the blame for the defeat for a poor kick out of defence that led to Williams's counter-attack.

Porta had already shown his class with wonderful tactical kicking from ball in hand and shrewd running into space and also praised scrum-half Adolfo Etchegaray, then a 34-year-old veteran of the 1965 tour of Africa, for the fine timing of his passes.

'When I kicked that loose ball through at the end I did not see JPR coming across but it was a silly chance to take,' Porta said. 'I could have kicked the ball off the field just as easily . . . [and] we would have won because there would have been no time for anyone to make a dangerous tackle.'

The late Wales international and *Observer* columnist Clem Thomas wrote: 'Surely Argentina must now be accorded full international recognition.'

Neither Wales in this Test nor England in a 13–13 draw with Argentina in 1978 at Twickenham awarded their players caps, though playing at full strength.

Argentina showed a rich vein of uninhibited back play while their eight-man shove in the scrum disconcerted their opponents.

Villegas became highly respected in Wales and was invited, along with other coaches from around the world, to speak on the game at the Welsh Rugby Union Centenary celebrations in 1980/81.

'[The scrum] isn't just a technical aspect of the game,' Villegas said in his speech. 'In this sense, the scrum must be considered a means and not an end. Every one of the forwards should be taught the following principle: the value of each forward to the team depends on his ability to add his effort to that of the pack.

And there is nothing better than the scrum to put this idea into practice. It's very important that any coach is quite clear about discipline being absolutely basic for the game of rugby.'

He said the scrum is the only facet of the game in which players are in physical contact before the ball comes into play. 'This contact has a special flavour and at the same time . . . a psychological effect which is basic for the rest of the match.

'I would like to emphasise my conviction that the true spirit of rugby in relation to the scrum means much more than just winning the ball.

'The real meaning of winning a scrum is not only to get the ball but also to push back the advantage line and the offside line and so defeat the opposing band physically and psychologically.

'You can still win a scrum without having obtained the ball.'

Welsh coaching director Ray Williams wrote an obituary on Villegas in 1988 in which he highlighted the Argentine performance in their narrow defeat by Wales at Cardiff Arms Park.

'The match was advertised as a Wales XV v Argentina but this was the strongest team that Wales could field; a team that was on the verge of four Triple Crowns in succession. On that day we were outplayed by the Pumas and the astute planning of Carlos Villegas,' Williams wrote.

Williams was the world's first professional coaching director, who held the post for more than a decade with the Welsh Rugby Union during a period when Wales set trends and standards in quality of play.

Veco had lost his position as Pumas coach two years previously despite recognition by the French that the Pumas scrum had got the better of theirs on their 1974 tour of Argentina.

Sebastian Perasso in his book *Veco Villegas, Pasión por el Rugby* wrote of France coach Toto Desclaux's admiration for the Pumas pack.

'The best thing that could have happened to the French team was that the Argentines were so dominant in the scrums they brought us down to earth. It was here in Buenos Aires that we learnt that the most brilliant attack can be held by a good scrum,' Desclaux said.

Then International Rugby Board chairman Danie Craven went further when he said: 'The Argentine Pumas are world masters of the scrum at the present moment and it's likely they are better than the 1974 Lions (who won the series against the Springboks 3–0).

'The San Isidro [scrummaging] system was one of the most important reasons for the tremendous improvement of the Pumas in their growing strength in world rugby, though not the only reason. Their rugby is flourishing in all aspects of the game and they can only blame themselves for losing last Saturday,' he said of the second Test against France.

Villegas and his team returned from Wales to little rest before facing New Zealand for the first time, losing the Tests 21–9 and 26–6.

He then had another shot at France when they toured Argentina with their Five Nations Grand Slam team in 1977.

The Pumas lost the first Test 26–3 but the second encounter turned into a kicking duel between Hugo Porta and Jean-Michel Aguirre and ended in an 18–18 draw, the first time the Pumas had not lost to France.

Midi Olympique reporter Henri Gatineau wrote that the French were lucky not to lose. 'Only Aguirre's precision saved us from defeat.'

A row with the UAR over his choice of captain for the South American Championship later that year led to Veco's resignation as Pumas coach but not the end of his influence at SIC.

SIX

CASI–SIC

WALK INTO CLUB Atlético San Isidro past the tennis courts on your right and the hockey pitch on the left and you are entering the stately premises of one of Argentina's most important sports clubs, in a suburb north of Buenos Aires known to sports lovers as the country's capital of rugby.

Further inside the grounds of the club founded in 1902 is the Spanish colonial-style clubhouse painted white with yellow trimmings and beyond that the first-team rugby pitch with a high concrete stand named La Catedral along part of one of the sides, painted in the same colours as the clubhouse.

The club is nearly 30 kilometres from the city centre at the corner of the main road out of Buenos Aires through the northern middle-class suburbs that line the banks of the Río de la Plata (River Plate) and the perpendicular road that leads to the racecourse at the Hipódromo de San Isidro.

Fans flocking to rugby matches at weekends walk along tree-lined cobbled streets and avenues of Spanish buildings where the wealthy settled in colonial times and English-style houses from the days when the British built the railways. Or they pass the cathedral, designed by French architects and opened in 1898, in the historic quarter.

Others also arrive virtually at the club gate by *colectivo*, typical Argentine buses, or train, walking the four blocks from San Isidro station, refurbished recently maintaining its British design and character.

The club was founded as a fusion of Club de Football San Isidro, made up of young men of Argentine families, and San Isidro Athletic Club, Britons who worked on the railways.

San Isidro is a bastion of tradition and conservatism so the club was rocked to the core by what appears today to have been a trivial incident of perceived misbehaviour in 1934 that produced a schism and the founding by breakaway players of San Isidro Club (SIC).

The acronyms of the two clubs are important and the way they are referred to in Argentina: CASI and SIC. The similarity of the two names has often confused foreign rivals as one or the other were often the club champions who played visiting teams in the days of long tours to Argentina.

SIC grew over the years into CASI's arch-rivals on the field and built a club on the outskirts of the suburb to rival them in support and influence but the contrast between the two when they founded their new club could not have been starker. SIC's new home, bought in 1939, was in a ditch.

They became known as *Los Zanjeros* (the ditch dwellers) because the grounds they bought for their new club had a ditch running through the middle and many locals, when they are going down to the club, say 'Voy a la zanja' (I'm going to the ditch).

The infamous incident occurred on 14 July 1934 during what Argentines call *el tercer tiempo* (third half) – in Spanish sports terminology the word *tiempo* (time) is the equivalent to half in English and the third 'half' is the traditional post-match get-together with opponents for drinks and/or dinner – at the CASI clubhouse after playing title rivals Gimnasia y Esgrima.

When one of the guests spilt his glass of wine over his trousers at dinner, he took them off and carried on eating. A CASI player nicknamed 'El Francés' (the Frenchman) said that as it was Bastille Day he would join him invoking the French revolutionaries known as *sansculottes* (without pants or trousers) and all the rest followed suit.

A non-rugby member of the club happened to see this and later reported the incident to the club authorities who suspended the 11 CASI first-team players involved for between one and two years.

Negotiations to try to explain what had happened and get lesser sanctions failed and more rugby members sided with the suspended players and refused to play in their respective (reserve, third and fourth) teams while selected juniors filled vacancies in the first team.

When the club president and board members were re-elected at the end of the year, the opposition broke away completely and set about founding a new club with 440 founder members including a majority of CASI's women's hockey players.

CASI had won 15 of their record 33 titles between 1917 and 1934 before the split within the club occurred.

It took CASI nearly a decade to recover from the loss of so many leading players and they did not win the title again until 1943. Since SIC came into existence they have won 25 titles to CASI's 18.

SEVEN

FRONT ROW

———————— 🐆 ————————

AUSTRALIAN RUGBY, WITH its fluidity and commitment to attack from all corners of the field, has been admired by Argentines, among them Daniel 'Huevo' Hourcade, the coach who took the Wallabies as his model for his exciting 2015 Pumas side that reached the World Cup semi-finals in England.

As early as Australia's first meeting with the Pumas on a two-Test tour of Argentina in 1979, the Wallabies' style caught the imagination of local fans as did the excitement generated by their own Pumas after promising recent performances against Wales, France and England.

Centre Rafael Madero, a Pumas debutant at Twickenham the previous year, scored two first-half tries for a 12–10 half-time lead in the first Test. After an exchange of penalties early in the second half, Hugo Porta secured a 24–13 victory with three drop goals. The Wallabies recovered to win the second Test 17–12.

'We had just returned from a tour of New Zealand where we had consolidated a team that was well respected,' Madero recalled many years later.

'From that match I began to admire Australia for their handling, above all in the backs with unexpected plays and moves. They have always been at the forefront with their daring on the edge of the gain line,' he said in the programme notes for the first of Argentina's 2020 Rugby Championship meetings with the Wallabies.

The next time the teams met was in a series in Australia in 1983, also shared 1–1 after the Pumas won the opener 18–3 in Brisbane, their first away win against a major rugby nation.

Coach Bob Dwyer's Wallabies won the second Test 29–13 in Sydney, with rising star David Campese scoring 13 points at full back.

However, the strongest early link between the two countries was in the front row with two notable props, Enrique 'Topo' Rodríguez and Patricio 'Pato' Noriega, emigrating to Australia and as a consequence both being capped first by their country of birth and later for the Wallabies.

Many years later, hooker Mario Ledesma became Michael Cheika's forwards coach for the 2015 World Cup where Australia reached the final after beating Argentina in the semi-finals.

Front-row forwards have been at the heart of Argentine rugby for half a century. Look back over the various best XVs at the earlier World Cups compiled by the organisers and media and even when the Pumas failed to reach the quarter-finals, several props and hookers are there.

Noriega and Federico Méndez in 1995, Ledesma in 1999 and 2007 were named as the best in their positions in such papers as Britain's *Sunday Times* and France's *L'Équipe*. Props Marcos Ayerza and Ramiro Herrera were named in the team of the 2015 tournament.

'At one time we made a very big difference in the scrum,' said Eduardo Fernández Gill, a former Pumitas (age group) coach who was appointed in 2019 to run a nationwide search for front-row forwards when Argentina found they had neglected this major asset while the Pumas sought a more expansive game.

'We exported props who were extraordinary ambassadors for Argentine rugby. [Other countries] became convinced that if they had Argentine props, they could have an Argentine scrum.'

The plan was to get Argentine scrums to work the way they

did before a spate of spinal injuries triggered a 2016 ban on scrums from pushing more than 1.5 metres and the introduction of Rugby Seguro (safe rugby), a programme of workshops aimed at avoiding serious injuries.

The ban was phased out in 2019 but the realisation, according to Fernández Gill, was that 'we have not been producing props as we should have done'.

Many Argentines of mainly Italian and Spanish extraction have an ideal build for front-row forwards, according to Ledesma, so it is not surprising they have long been sought after.

Topo Rodríguez played in four series between the two nations, two against the Pumas after moving to Australia in 1984: a comfortable 2–0 win for the Wallabies on home soil in 1986 (39–19 in the first Test, during which Porta was injured, and 26–0 in the second) and a 1–0 loss in Buenos Aires in 1987 (19–19 and 27–19 to the Pumas).

Nearly a decade later, Rodríguez was followed to Australia and into the Wallabies' team by Noriega after he had played for the Pumas at the 1995 World Cup, also lending his considerable nous as a scrummager to his adopted country.

Top front-row forwards emerged from the provincial unions as much as they did in Buenos Aires with Topo Rodríguez, who played for Australia at the inaugural World Cup in 1987, coming from Córdoba.

Roberto Grau and Federico Méndez both came from Mendoza and played in South Africa and Europe. They were followed by Omar Hasan from Tucumán, who played in New Zealand, Australia and France.

Méndez, the first player to win two European Cup titles, first with Bath in 1998 then Northampton in 2000, was the first professional to break Argentina's ban when he was deemed essential for a home series against the then world champion Springboks in 1996 while playing for Natal in South Africa. He had already won 30 of his 73 caps by then.

This angered the amateur lobby in Buenos Aires but pleased

the chief provincial unions like Méndez's Mendoza. UAR president Luis Gradín saw the need to end the restrictions if Argentina were to avoid falling behind the leading teams and Mauricio Reggiardo, who had joined Castres in France, soon followed, recalled against England.

The second Pumas front-row forward to go abroad after Rodríguez was loose-head prop Serafín Dengra, who played in the Pumas side that beat South Africa as the South American Jaguars in 1982 and drew with New Zealand in 1985.

While it would take another decade for the world game to turn professional, Dengra received two suspensions from the UAR, the first for six months when he joined Australian club Wests Bulldogs in 1985 and was also selected for Queensland.

Having returned home the following year and played for Argentina at the 1987 World Cup, taking his total caps to 21, Dengra joined Rovigo in Italy, where a number of Argentines were enticed with disguised earnings, and had his Pumas career ended by a four-year ban.

The flow of top props and hookers grew in the new millennium with Marcos 'Toro' Ayerza going to Leicester Tigers where he lined up alongside Martin Castrogiovanni, the best of several Argentine-born forwards who played for Italy, and stayed for more than a decade.

Ayerza and Juan Figallo, who was from Salta and played for Montpellier and Saracens, both took part in three World Cups.

In the professional era Argentina beat Australia three more times up to and including the 2021 Rugby Championship, for a record of six wins and three draws, two of these in that tournament, in 36 meetings.

Foundation

ARGENTINE RUGBY HAS always looked after its own, during their playing careers and afterwards, and for a long time has been supporting players who suffered serious injuries that forced them to retire from the game prematurely.

This support became more public and organised under the Argentine union's foundation (Fundación de la Unión Argentina de Rugby: FUAR), created five years ago with former Puma Ricardo Handley as president.

Handley, one of the original Pumas in the side that toured southern Africa in 1965, talks of his pride in being the foundation's president and the incredible impression these injured players, many of them confined to wheelchairs, have made on him, calling them his heroes.

'The FUAR was founded about five years ago. It existed before that, but what happened was that Pichot and the people of the UAR decided they should treat this seriously and accept they had at that time about 35 seriously injured players. It was kind of treated under the rug as people didn't like to talk about it because it could scare families from sending their kids to play rugby.

'It was a big step in the right direction. Pichot was very much involved in this. I made friends with him when I was manager of the Pumas and he called me to ask if I wanted to preside the FUAR and I said yes.

'We organised it and it really helps these guys when they get injured, to cover expenses, to adapt their homes and then gives them a monthly amount to help them to have a better lifestyle and we buy them equipment so they can use their computers, their iPhones, those who can't use their hands or their arms, and we're very much in contact with them every month to see how they're doing, what their needs are.

'The FUAR is economically solid and the players with serious injuries really appreciate what the FUAR does for them. It also helps players with not such serious injuries who might need an operation or treatment and don't have medical cover. About 40 per cent of people in Argentina don't have insurance.'

Part of the membership that players at all the clubs in the country pay every year goes to the foundation. The UAR also pays a percentage of its earnings into the foundation to cover publicity costs.

'And we have an annual dinner that has become not just for the injured players but the annual Argentine rugby dinner. It's in benefit of these guys but it's turned out to be quite something and people come from all over the country. We now have nearly 1,000 members of the foundation who pay a monthly fee.'

The injuries sustained mainly by front-row forwards, three in a single season in 2016, led to important changes in scrummaging regulations in Argentina, whose Pumas earned a worldwide reputation in the 1970s for their strength and technique in the scrum.

'Scrummaging suffered because the rules in Argentina were different and also at the time of the *bajadita* it was dangerous because scrums were set very low and they collapsed often.'

In 2016, pushing was banned altogether at lower junior level while it was limited to at most 1.5 metres at senior level except for five-metre scrums.

This had a detrimental effect on the Pumas pack, something coach Mario Ledesma, a world-class hooker in his playing days, set about trying to rectify, saying they needed to recover their DNA, after giving away three tries from scrums in a Test defeat in Ireland in 2018 when he took charge of the Pumas.

'Being president of the FUAR is fantastic; it permits me to give back a lot of what rugby gave me and it's tough also to see how these people live.

'I would say they're my heroes because they play a Test match every morning. They have to live with that and survive and be very strong; they are incredible people, people who love rugby. You'd think they would say shit rugby, this is what happened to me for playing rugby, but they love the sport, it's incredible.'

Handley believes that all rules which improve safety in the game are essential.

'There's much more consciousness of the dangers and the rules have changed to not permit certain actions, especially in the front rows, to take advantage of the opposition. I think the players nowadays have realised there has to be more fair play in terms of scrummaging which before didn't exist.'

EIGHT

FRANCE

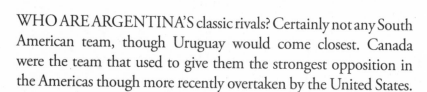

WHO ARE ARGENTINA'S classic rivals? Certainly not any South American team, though Uruguay would come closest. Canada were the team that used to give them the strongest opposition in the Americas though more recently overtaken by the United States.

It could be South Africa as the closest of the rugby powers geographically and because of the long-standing relationship between the two nations.

England, as much as in football, have been the team to beat if only because of their standing as creators of the game.

But it has to be France, with their similar passion for the game as Latins, because they did the most to encourage Argentine progress in the amateur era and then aided them in the professional age when so many Pumas joined French clubs.

'They were the country we measured ourselves against to see where we stood,' said lock Chapa Branca, who had many battles with French forwards in the 1970s and '80s.

During a particularly violent series in Buenos Aires in 1985 there was a free-for-all from the kick-off in the second Test when the rival packs charged into each other without much concern for winning the ball.

'There was that time when no one went for the ball at the kick-off,' said Branca, implying the forwards were targeting each other to get in the first hits and weaken their rivals psychologically.

'The fact is that if you don't impose yourself psychologically coming from [rugby's] second tier you get thumped. That's where that [often quoted] phrase of mine came from: "If the other guy was crazy you had to be one and a half times crazy."'

Argentina had won the first Test 24–16, their first-ever victory over France, and the visiting team were out for revenge having been overcome in the forwards.

The visiting team's blood was already up before an unfortunate event happened to the Pumas that was not of the players' making.

The bus that was to transport the team the 40 kilometres into the city from their camp on the outskirts wouldn't start and they were about 40 minutes late rushing to the Ferro Carril Oeste ground in several cars and changing on the way.

'When we got to Ferro, the French were already changed and waiting for us, swearing at us, and that's when it got out of hand,' Branca said. 'We dropped our bags and started punching each other.

'That's what led to the fight on the pitch. You can't let yourself get overrun or you'll disappear from the match.'

France won the second Test 23–15 and drew the series.

The Pumas coaches said that in their planning they had envisaged Argentina winning the second Test, not the first, but after 20 minutes of the first the previous weekend, when they saw three French players on the ground after a maul they looked at each other and understood that was their day.

Branca still has a place in his heart for the French and speaks highly of men like the Spanish-speaking full back Serge Blanco – who ensured they all shook hands again at a French embassy reception afterwards – and his opposite number in the second row, Alain Lorieux.

'The rivalry was on the pitch but they respected us because we'd gained their respect.'

Brilliant France centre Philippe Sella said: 'I played against the Argentine team 11 times. It's a classic . . .

'There's a rivalry like with England, only not the same. It's a rivalry between Latin teams, with players who can understand each other.'

The French were not the first to tour Argentina, who entertained British teams in the early part of the last century, but they became the most frequent visitors from their first tour in 1949.

France may lead their head-to-head record with 38 wins and one draw in 53 meetings but Argentina lead 10–9 in meetings this century up to a November Test at the Stade de France in 2021.

In the Hugo Porta era, which began in 1971 when the legendary fly-half made his debut against Chile in the South American Championship, the rivalry became well established and Argentina tougher opponents.

With Porta as the new Pumas captain in 1977, having lost the first Test 26–3 in a series in Buenos Aires, Argentina held France to an 18–18 draw in the second which the French readily conceded they were lucky not to lose.

Eight years later, Argentina had one of their best seasons with their first victory over the French preceding a tour by New Zealand in which the Pumas almost beat the All Blacks who held on for a 21–21 draw in the second Test.

Argentina, drawing larger crowds with each exploit, had moved their Test matches from Gimnasia y Esgrima to the 24,000-capacity Ferro Carril Oeste (western railway) football stadium from Ireland's visit in 1970.

As the Pumas' fan base increased throughout the 1970s, Ferro was more and more packed for Test matches with a very real worry about whether the wooden stands facing the concrete main tribune would withstand the jumping up and down in unison of their chanting, passionate supporters.

The next time France toured in 1986, Argentina moved to the larger stadium of first division football club Vélez Sarsfield, which holds 50,000 people after being modernised for the FIFA World Cup in 1978.

That series was also shared, Argentina winning 15–13 then losing 22–9, and so was yet another in 1988 (15–18 and 18–6) but later that year France won 2–0 at home (29–9 and 28–18).

As the gap widened between the Argentine amateur game and the leading nations already edging closer to open professionalism, the Pumas lost the next home series in 1992 (27–12 and 33–9).

Yet the French were stunned later that year, and totally against the odds, when the Pumas upset them 24–20 in Nantes.

The next time France travelled to Argentina was after the World Cup in 1995 for the four-nation Latin Cup, an initiative to give more exposure to second-tier teams with Italy and Romania also taking part and which the French won, beating the Pumas 47–12 in the final.

The French won a series in Buenos Aires in 1996 and hosted the second Latin Cup in the south of France in October 1997, again beating the Pumas in the decider, this time 32–27.

France won another series (35–18 and 37–12) in Argentina in 1998 and later that year beat the Pumas 34–14 in Nantes on their tour of Europe.

The teams' first World Cup clash was a 47–26 quarter-final victory for the French in Dublin in 1999 after the Pumas had upset Ireland in a play-off in Lens to reach the last eight for the first time.

The new century brought better results for Argentina in this classic rivalry with a 28–27 home victory in 2002 and a first home series win the following year (10–6 and 33–32).

The Pumas became more familiar with French ways as more of them joined clubs in France.

With series becoming rarer and teams playing one-off Tests on tours of several countries in the June and November Test windows, Argentina won 24–14 in Marseille in 2004, a fourth consecutive victory, but lost 27–26 in Paris in 2006 following their first away victory over England at Twickenham.

Their next clash was in the opening match of the 2007 World Cup at the Stade de France, Argentina's shock 17–12 victory that upset predictions in a pool that also included Ireland.

The Pumas and France met again at the Parc des Princes in the third-place play-off and Argentina ratified their rich vein of form winning 34–10 which put their record for the century against the French at six wins to one during Marcelo Loffreda's tenure as Pumas coach.

France gained a modicum of revenge in 2008 with a 12–6 home victory in Marseille, lost 41–13 on their next trip to Buenos Aires in 2010 but won again 15–9 in Montpellier later in the year.

A 2012 French tour of northern Argentina yielded a 23–20 defeat in Córdoba and a 49–10 victory in Tucumán.

The Pumas, who had joined the southern hemisphere's Rugby Championship in 2012, lost to France 39–22 in Lille during their November tour of Europe that year but won 18–13 in Paris in 2014.

The next time the teams played a series, in Tucumán in 2016, it was shared with Argentina winning 30–19 then being crushed 27–0.

Drawn together in a tough pool which also included England at the 2019 World Cup in Japan, they met in their opening match with France running up a 20–3 half-time lead against a strangely disorientated Argentina.

The Pumas were a different team after the break and very nearly won but a drop kick from replacement fly-half Camille Lopez secured a 23–21 victory for France.

NINE

THE BRITISH

ARGENTINA PLAYED THEIR first international match in 1910 against a Combined British touring team recently accorded Lions status by World Rugby along with subsequent visits in 1927 and 1936.

The Tour was organised by the River Plate Rugby Union, predecessor of the Unión Argentina de Rugby (UAR), as part of Argentina's celebrations of the centenary of the May Revolution, the event that sparked the colony's push for independence from Spain, which was declared in July 1816.

The British visitors, mostly English with three Scots, won the Test 28–3 against the Argentine side made up entirely of English names including at number 8 former South African captain Barry Heatlie, who had led the Springboks to their first series win over the British Isles in 1903 before moving to Argentina where he lived for 20 years.

The Lions returned to Argentina in 1927 and played four international matches, comfortably winning all of them and conceding only three points. The Argentines played for the first time in the colours they have since been famous for, sky blue and white hoops.

The British played another match in Buenos Aires in 1936, winning 23–0.

Meanwhile, the domestic game was progressing, attracting more and more players who were not of British origin.

Ireland were the first of the British Isles nations to tour Argentina in 1952. The tour was almost cancelled due to the death of Eva Perón but as the team were already on their way to South America it went ahead with the first match in Chile followed by eight in Argentina. The Irish won the Test series with a 3–3 draw and a 6–0 win.

Further contact with Britain was maintained by tours of a combined Oxford and Cambridge Universities side, which included British international players, in 1948, 1956, 1965 and 1971.

One of the Cambridge University students in the combined team in 1948 was Barry Holmes, who was in fact returning home since he had been born in Buenos Aires to English parents and brought up there, educated at St George's College in the suburb of Quilmes.

The Holmes family was part of the British community that introduced a wide range of sports, notably football, rugby and polo, to Argentina in the second half of the 19th century when Britain was strongly influential in the economic development of the country.

Holmes, who played six Test matches at full back, returned to Buenos Aires again the following year having turned out for England four times in the 1949 Five Nations Championship while finishing his studies.

He played for Old Georgians that season and was picked by Argentina to face France, who were making their first tour of the country, in two Tests in August to mark the 50th anniversary of the Argentine union, to the surprise of members of the French team who recalled him playing against them for England at Twickenham earlier in the year.

There was a tragic end to this remarkable final year of Holmes's life. The 21-year-old married in November and went to work as a surveyor in Salta in the Andean north-west of the country where he fell ill with typhoid within a week and died.

Wales, Scotland and Ireland all sent touring teams in the late 1960s but did not award caps for the matches until they were sure of what they were facing; and what they faced surprised them – or at least that was the Argentine view.

'There was discomfort among the British because they said Argentina didn't play within the rules of the game,' Papuchi Guastella, a former Argentina fly-half and later coach, said in *Ser Puma*, a history of the Pumas. They were unhappy that Argentina could play them as equals, he said.

Wales, captained by the legendary John Dawes and with other, future greats like Phil Bennett and JPR Williams in their squad, lost 9–5 and drew 9–9 in 1968.

Scotland lost 20–3 and won 6–3 in 1969 and Ireland, with Willie John McBride in their pack, were beaten 8–3 and 6–3 in 1970.

The Welsh toured with an official coach for the first time, as noted in an article by JBG Thomas, chief rugby writer for the *Western Mail*, published in the programme for the 1976 match against Argentina in Cardiff.

'It was the first for Clive Rowlands as a coach, as a result of a WRU change of heart in the matter of official coaches and while Rowlands had to learn the job en route, as it were, it set him off on a successful career as a coach, ending with a Triple Crown and Grand Slam for Wales (in 1971). For this, indeed, the Argentine tour played a part and ensured that coaching of national XVs in the British Isles became a necessity.'

The Oxbridge team were beaten for the first time 9–3 following a 19–19 draw in the opening game on the 1965 tour which came a few months after Argentina's landmark tour of Africa. Argentina then won both matches, 11–3 and 6–3, in the 1971 Oxbridge tour, the last of its kind.

Twickenham 1978

ENGLAND CANCELLED A planned tour in 1973 because of the political unrest in Argentina and met the Pumas for the first time in 1978 when an England XV were held to a 13–13 draw at Twickenham.

Argentina, who were celebrating their football World Cup victory amid world condemnation of the country's military dictatorship, travelled to England with a new team who were met by demonstrations against the regime's torture and disappearance of dissidents.

'It wasn't at all easy,' said team captain Hugo Porta. 'Women were being handed leaflets telling them to be careful of speaking to us – that we came from a country where torture reigned.'

The refusal of the UAR to accept Arturo Rodríguez Jurado as the coaches' choice of captain for the 1977 South American Championship in the absence of Porta, who was away in France, led to them – Veco Villegas and Gringo Perasso – resigning and ten players being suspended after quitting the team in protest.

Guastella, who had coached the 1965 team that went to South Africa, took charge again and picked a side with only two survivors from the 1976 tour to Wales: Porta and full back Martín Sansot.

Half the team made their Pumas debuts at Twickenham including centre Marcelo Loffreda, who went on to enjoy a fine, long playing and coaching career that reached its zenith with the 2007 World Cup bronze medal.

The tour also marked Pochola Silva's return after his suspension for being involved in an advertisement in 1972 in contravention of the UAR's strict amateur rules.

Alfredo Soares Gache was due to partner Porta at half back but missed the Test through suspension after – belying his nickname 'Bambi' – he was sent off near the end of the victory over North

Midlands at Moseley for punching an opponent during a free-for-all. Ricardo Landajo took his place.

Argentina were 3–0 down to a John Horton drop goal when Porta unexpectedly decided against kicking a penalty and took a quick tap. He slipped through a gap in the defence and fed Marcelo Campo who was charging along beside him and, faced by a wall of defenders, the wing leapt over them to score a memorable try.

Chris Gifford's try restored England's lead but the Pumas scored again from a lineout. Gabriel Travaglini palmed a long throw to the back of the line to giant lock Alejandro Iachetti who broke through and was backed up by flanker Tomas Petersen who in turn fed scorer Ricardo Passaglia.

Peter Squires then scored a try converted by Kevin Bushell to put England ahead again with Porta's penalty on the hour mark levelling the score.

England were awarded a penalty with the clock running down the seconds and Porta complained only for referee Clive Norling to give England ten yards.

'I wanted the earth to swallow me up,' said Porta, whose ambition like that of most Argentines has always been to beat the inventors of the game and now feared defeat. But Bushell missed.

It was a wonderful result for Argentina and Guastella said: 'Hugo was already a star, but there he made the leap [to greatness].'

Argentina, whose victory over Australia in 1979 was their first in a match against a major nation in which both teams were awarded caps, believed they had a good chance to beat England when Bill Beaumont's side toured the country in 1981.

But after a 19–19 draw in the first Test they were frustrated by a strong defensive performance from the visiting side and lost 12–6.

England prepared tactics to try to nullify the very real threat posed by Porta and he had a rare poor game for Argentina having set his heart on a victory.

It proved a disappointing experience for Porta, who uncharacteristically lost his cool with a dangerous tackle on his opposite number Huw Davies for which he was penalised and received a warning from the referee.

The Malvinas/Falklands War in 1982 led to eight years without Tests against the British teams until England, minus half their Five Nations side, visited Argentina on a 1990 tour marked by anti-British sentiment in the crowds and brawls on the pitch.

'It wasn't the sport we know now; it was properly Wild West,' hooker John Olver said. 'I remember all the team talks weren't about "we are going to do this and we are going to do that", it was "right, we are going to kick the shit out of them". The common saying was that "we are going to let our metal do the talking". That was in the days that rucking was allowed and you would really rake someone on your side of the ruck to physically impose yourself. Thank God that has stopped now because it was brutal.'

Porta had retired from Test rugby in 1987 so he missed that series although he led his club Banco Nación, the Buenos Aires first division champions, to a memorable 29–21 victory over England in the opening tour match.

England also lost to Buenos Aires and Cuyo (Mendoza) but shared the Test series, winning the first 25–12 then losing 15–13 with an overall try count of four to nil for the touring side.

The first Test was prop Jason Leonard's debut at the start of a career that would end 14 years later with a record haul of 114 England caps. His first three Tests were against Argentina, both matches at Vélez and the 51–0 romp against a new, young Pumas side at Twickenham later in the year.

Leonard's first taste of rugby in Argentina came in the second match of the tour against Tucumán, whose team were called 'La Naranja' (orange) and noted as uncompromising and sometimes violent opposition having fought battles with France and the New Zealand Maori team.

'Tucumán had a big reputation of intimidation of touring teams but they were also one of the regions that had the biggest losses in the Falklands War,' Leonard said in 2020. 'That's why tempers were running high and the rugby was brutal in those days.'

Armed soldiers lined the perimeter fence and fans burnt a Union Jack.

Leonard, whose Atlas Foundation supports social inclusion projects in Argentina, added: 'While tempers were running high on the pitch, off it Argentina was a wonderfully hospitable country to experience and I am still in touch with Diego Cash who propped against me in the second Test of that 1990 tour.'

After some dour performances against England with all their points coming from penalties converted by wing Hernán Vidou, usually a half back who was in the side mainly for his place-kicking skill, the Pumas changed coach, Luis Gradín taking over from Michingo O'Reilly.

Gradín asked the 39-year-old Porta to come out of international retirement for one more tour to the British Isles at the end of the year to help blood a new generation.

Argentina had banned players who were playing abroad from all rugby, notably those lured to Italy by 'professional' terms – accommodation, pocket money, fees for studies.

These players included Diego Domínguez, the brilliant fly-half who should have been groomed as Porta's successor and lost patience with the Pumas' coaches. Another to leave was Fabio Gómez, who had shared a half-back partnership with Porta at their club Banco Nación.

The tour, which began with a narrow 20–18 loss to Ireland, turned into a nightmare with a 51–0 defeat by a full-strength England team captained by Will Carling that was building momentum for a shot at the World Cup title the following year.

Teenage prop Federico Méndez, one of many players making their Pumas debut on the tour, was sent off near the end for stunning Paul Ackford with a punch after mistaking him for Jeff Probyn, with whom he had tussled moments earlier.

'I was young then, 18 years old, and inexperienced,' Méndez said in a 1995 interview. 'It was a mistake. I had my punishment and I learned from it. I reacted in a minute of blind rage and punched the England player closest to me after Jeff Probyn stamped on me.'

Porta, who was carrying an injury, bowed out permanently midway through the first half of another rout, 49–3 to Scotland, the reigning Five Nations Grand Slam champions, at Murrayfield.

The next time Argentina met England was in Durban in their opening pool match at the 1995 World Cup in South Africa.

Many of the raw Pumas of the 1990 tour had matured despite the strictures hampering the team's development in the grey area between an amateur game and impending professionalism and run up plenty of caps in the school of hard knocks against most of the top nations.

Between the second Test win against England in Buenos Aires in August 1990 and the World Cup match in Durban five years later, the Pumas had won three Tests out of 18 against the top teams, a shock upset of France in Nantes in 1992 and a series win over Scotland in Buenos Aires in 1994.

However, with the best front row of the tournament in tight head Pato Noriega, hooker Federico Méndez and Matías Corral, Argentina gave England a good game and scored two tries to none but England won 24–18 with all their points coming from Rob Andrew's boot.

Argentina could have won their next meeting at Twickenham 18 months later, losing 20–18 to an England side brimming with talent but performing poorly. Leonard scored the only try six minutes from time in the only Test of a seven-match tour.

Prop Mauricio Reggiardo, who had joined Castres in France earlier in the year, became the second professional to be picked by Argentina. The UAR had ended more than 20 years of banning players based abroad when they included Méndez in a Test series at home to South Africa a month earlier despite being on the books of Natal.

The following season began for the Pumas with a home series against England, losing the first Test 46–20 but winning the second 33–13.

The frequency of meetings continued into the new century with Argentina, now under coach Marcelo 'Tano' Loffreda, losing 19–0 in London in 2000 and 26–18 in Buenos Aires in 2002.

Twickenham 2006

AS LOFFREDA'S TEAM, led by Agustín Pichot, built towards Argentina's best World Cup performance, they beat England for the first time at Twickenham in November 2006.

The teams shared a series in 2009, with the Pumas winning the second Test 24–22 in Salta after England had taken the first 37–15 at Old Trafford in Manchester a week earlier, where Argentina played hosts. England also won a November Test at Twickenham 16–9 that year.

Their 2011 World Cup meeting in Dunedin was a close affair with England winning 13–9 in their opening pool match but the Pumas still reached the last eight following a 13–12 victory against Scotland before losing to hosts New Zealand.

There were also three meetings in 2013, including a series in Salta and Buenos Aires, all won convincingly by England.

England continued to hold the upper hand in the Eddie Jones era, starting with a 27–14 victory at Twickenham in November 2016 despite losing wing Elliot Daly to a red card in the fifth minute for a dangerous tackle on Leonardo Senatore.

Jones's side made the better start despite being a man down, a penalty try amid a string of infringements by the Pumas helping them to open up a 16–0 half-time lead.

Hardly had the second half got under way when Argentina hit back with a quick brace of tries from Facundo Isa and Santiago Cordero.

England then held firm, added two Owen Farrell penalties and Jonny May raced away for the decisive try with 12 minutes remaining. The teams ended level in numbers after replacement prop Enrique Pieretto was sent off near the end for stamping.

England won an exciting series 2–0 the following June in Argentina which constituted an upset.

Jones had lost 17 first-choice players to the British and Irish Lions touring New Zealand at the same time and toured with 18 uncapped players in a 37–man squad while Argentina were at home and at full strength with the whole squad contracted to the Jaguares Super Rugby franchise.

The Pumas appeared to have the first Test in San Juan in the bag, an exhilarating end-to-end match in which they were leading the try count 4–3 and were 34–31 ahead in the dying minutes.

But replacement wing Denny Solomona, making his Test debut, burst through the cover to score the winning try for a 38–34 victory. Man of the match George Ford scored 23 points including a try.

England won an equally exciting second Test 35–25 in Santa Fe edging the try count 4–3 and with another fine kicking performance from fly-half Ford.

The matches could have gone either way with Argentina coach Daniel Hourcade favouring the attacking game that had taken his side to the 2015 World Cup semi-finals while England newcomers like Tom Curry were looking to find a place in Jones's 2019 World Cup plans.

Facing Argentina in a Lions tour year was a good move for England because the Pumas could guarantee first-rate opposition and defeat would not be a major setback in Jones's World Cup planning while wins were a bonus.

Jones's side won 21–8 when they met again at Twickenham five months later and Hourcade's days were numbered. He resigned after losing a home series to Wales in June 2018.

When the teams met in their pool match at the 2019 World Cup in Japan, England won comfortably 39–10 after lock Tomás Lavanini was sent off for a dangerous tackle on Owen Farrell midway through the first half leaving the Pumas a player short, too big a handicap against the title favourites.

TEN

PORTA

HUGO PORTA'S CROWNING glory could be said to have come not in the sky blue and white colours of Argentina but as leader of the South American Jaguars, the Pumas in all but name, against South Africa when they memorably beat the Springboks 21–12 in the second Test of their 1982 tour.

Many of Argentina's brilliant results in the 1970s and '80s were inspired by the great fly-half and cemented by the Pumas' pack.

It often turned into ten-man rugby with a lot of tackling by a back division not given too much scope to play the ball out, though thrilling when they got the chance to counter-attack.

Yet such was Porta's creative ability and deceptive running that whenever he saw a half chance he could dart through the tightest defences and bring his backs into play to great effect.

He was not a fan of the ten-man game or the predominance some coaching gurus in Argentina gave to scrummaging, a renowned Argentine strength, but for practical purposes he often had to play to his strengths as a kicker for the Pumas to have a chance of winning Tests.

Porta came to play at fly-half by chance. When he was first

called up to the Pumas under coach Angel Guastella for the 1971 South American Championship it was as a scrum-half.

'We were in a practice and the fly-halves were injured . . . Guastella, a former international fly-half, asked: "Are you up to playing number 10?" I answered: "Explain it to me and I'll have a go."'

The wily Guastella, coach since the groundbreaking 1965 tour of South Africa and a promoter of open, attacking rugby, could well have already seen the promise in Porta as a playmaker and sought an opportunity to put his gut feeling to the test.

Porta made his debut at fly-half in a 20–3 win over Chile in October 1971 at the age of 20 in Montevideo, where Uruguay hosted the tournament, and never looked back.

It is surprising given his prolific scoring throughout his career that he did not contribute any points in that match but he got off the mark with a penalty in the next, a 50–6 rout of Brazil, and ended the five-team tournament adding three tries, three drop goals and two conversions.

'From that moment and for nearly 18 years I wore the number 10. From something unexpected, what happened changed my life forever,' said Porta, Argentina's greatest player and widely regarded as the best fly-half of the 1980s.

Porta scored 590 Test points in his career, an Argentine record that stood until it was surpassed by Felipe Contepomi, who also made his debut against Chile in 1998 and amassed 651 until his retirement in 2013. The record was broken by active Pumas fly-half Nicolás Sánchez who had passed 800 by 2021.

Standout results of the Porta era

1976: Wales 20 Argentina 19. The day Argentina almost upset the world's top team who were a Wales XV in name but at full strength. Porta kicked one penalty and one conversion.

1977: Argentina 18 France 18. A kicking duel between Jean-Michel Aguirre and Porta with six penalties apiece in the second Test, ending a run of ten Test defeats against top nations. France won the first Test 26–3 with the Pumas' points coming from a Porta penalty.

1978: The 13–13 draw at Twickenham was theoretically against an England XV but it was England at full strength in practice. Porta had the final word with a penalty on the hour, to add to his earlier conversion, after two tries apiece, although England could have won but missed a penalty in added time.

1979: A 24–13 victory over Australia in Buenos Aires in the countries' first ever meeting. Argentina won the try count 2–1 in a tight first half and a hat-trick of drop goals by Porta in the final 22 minutes secured the win. He also kicked both conversions and a penalty.

The Wallabies had their revenge, winning the second Test 17–12 a week later when Porta kicked a penalty, a conversion and a drop goal.

1981: Argentina 19 England 19. Bill Beaumont's side were held in the first Test but won the second 12–6 on England's first tour of Argentina. Porta scored a penalty, a conversion and a drop goal in the first Test and converted flanker Gabriel Travaglini's try in the second.

1983: Australia 3 Argentina 18. A first away win over a top tier nation with Porta kicking ten points from two conversions, a penalty and a drop goal. The Wallabies hit back to win the second Test 29–13 with Porta contributing two penalties and a drop for the Pumas.

1985: Argentina 24 France 16. Argentina's first win over France, scoring two tries and Porta kicking two conversions and a drop goal to take a 15–6 lead into the second half. Then Porta kept the Pumas ahead with three penalties despite two French tries.

They shared the series after France won the second Test 23–15. Porta converted Diego Cuesta Silva's try and kicked three penalties.

1985: Argentina 21 New Zealand 21. The All Blacks scored four tries to two to win the first Test 33–20 when Porta kicked three penalties and a drop goal for the Pumas but, much to the great All Blacks flanker Murray Mexted's consternation, they only drew the second.

New Zealand ran in four tries to none, all in the first half, and led 18–9 at the interval but conceded a hat-trick of drop goals to Porta, who had already kicked four penalties. The Pumas could have won but for a knock-on by number 8 Ernesto Ure on the line at the end. Ure was disconsolate afterwards.

1987: Argentina 27 Australia 19. After a disappointing World Cup in New Zealand in the southern hemisphere autumn, Argentina won a home series against Australia after drawing the first Test 19–19 with Porta scoring four penalties and a drop goal.

Porta steered the Pumas to victory with five penalties, two drop goals and a conversion in the second Test against an Australian side that included Michael Lynagh and former Pumas prop Topo Rodríguez.

'I needed this personal comeback. I felt so bad after the World Cup,' said Porta.

1990: Banco Nación 29 England 21. Porta, who had retired from Test rugby at the end of 1987, finally got the win he craved against England, inspiring the Argentine club champions to victory over the first British team to tour the country since the 1982 Malvinas/Falklands War.

Porta was persuaded by Argentina's coach Luis Gradín to come out of international retirement at the age of 39 later that year to lead a young, new Pumas side on a tour of Ireland and Britain in which they lost 20–18 in Dublin before being trounced by England and Five Nations Grand Slam champions Scotland.

Jaguars

NO MENTION OF Porta can go without an account of his brilliance as captain and inspiration of a South America XV, nicknamed the Jaguars, in Tests against the Springboks and the heights he reached in the second Test in 1982.

Porta scored a full house of points as he led the disguised full Pumas side to a 21–12 victory in Bloemfontein after losing the first Test 50–18 in Pretoria.

While taking part in the first Jaguars tour of South Africa in 1980, Porta was invited to play for the South African Barbarians against the British and Irish Lions during their tour later in the year. The Barbarians lost the match in Durban 25–14, but Porta's performance drew huge praise from Welsh coach Carwyn James who was among the media representatives covering the match.

'Everything that happened around Hugo Porta was contested at a much lower level of skill and intellectual awareness,' James wrote. 'For a critic or coach or ex fly-half it was a question of having one's faith restored in the aesthetic and artistic possibilities of back play.

'The dexterity of his passing makes his opposite number look slow and cumbersome. Porta's ambling, loping running bemused the Lions' back row who thought they had him covered but found that they could not lay a hand on him.'

The Jaguars tours were controversial, breaking the boycott imposed on South Africa because of the country's policy of racial segregation. The Argentine government had joined the international boycott and refused the UAR permission to send the Pumas on tour to South Africa.

The Pumas got round the issue by travelling disguised as the Jaguars, with Chilean, Uruguayan and Paraguayan players in their squad, although the Tests were contested by fifteen Argentines.

Porta's special relationship with South Africa led to his being appointed as Argentina's ambassador to Pretoria by President Carlos Menem, serving from 1991 to 1995.

Porta said in 1995 that he didn't regret playing the Springboks with the Jaguars because 'it was one of the ways of contributing to apartheid being abolished. Sport was made to unite [people].'

Porta, having retired at 36 in 1987, then again at 39 in 1990, finally had his testimonial match just short of his 48th birthday in 1999, the year Argentina made their World Cup breakthrough by reaching the quarter-finals for the first time.

The Pumas beat the Rest of the World 49–31 in their first match of the year with Agustín Pichot, soon to be the game's new icon in Argentina, at half back with Porta, who played for the opening 18 minutes during which he kicked his last international conversion.

A look back

'I PLAYED MY best rugby between 1978 and 1983. I think I was at the height of my powers in that era and accompanied, of course, by great players. During that period the Pumas had some great results in the history of Argentine rugby.

'We also had the chance to go to South Africa, not as the Pumas but a South America XV and that meant we could compete with the Springboks and, more than anything, help them get out of that situation in which South African rugby found itself.

'South Africa is a country with a special place in my heart because of the opportunities to play with the best, to take part in the country's transitition to democracy, to meet President Mandela and to have my family accompany me in that experience at the embassy re-establishing diplomatic relations between Argentina and South Africa.

'I believe sport is a bridge between different countries, between different generations and between different civilisations. The richness of the rugby that one played was not only on the field but also in the experiences off the pitch, being able to get to know the customs and the way of life in other countries and represent my country with the values it instilled in me as ambassador. I think every sportsperson is an ambassador of their country.'

Such were his ball skills that Porta might have become a footballer instead of a 'rugbier'.

'In Argentina, as you know, football is the sport we all play. In my time, I played it in the street, at school and the ball is always present in one's infancy and youth. I started going to my club at a very young age, Banco Nación, which was the only club I played for because the social aspect of club life has a very important place in Argentina. We didn't just develop there as athletes but also socially; we also made friends there and in my case I met my wife there too so my family always went to the club.

'At the moment I decided I wanted to play rugby, my father tried in many ways to prevent me from doing so for fear that I might get badly hurt. I was taken to some clubs for football trials, but I had made my decision. Later on when I was older, other chances arose but I was focused on rugby. But I would have liked to have been a footballer, no doubt.'

Argentina's two biggest clubs and arch-rivals, Boca Juniors and River Plate, were both interested.

'I had a trial at River and when I was older, 24 or 25, I'd play games with former footballers and the people of Boca saw me and tried to entice me to go and train with them but I was already well into rugby.'

Playing in and for Argentina, not a major rugby nation during his time, Porta suffered plenty of defeats and disappointments as well as days of glory.

'During such a long career, it wasn't all victories and I believe the road to success is paved with many falls. I always say I lost much more than I won if we're talking of matches because I am from a club where rugby is not very traditional, a small club, and I often lost by lots of points, but that helped me develop in adversity.

'The first World Cup was a huge frustration for all of us who went there with greater expectations but couldn't get past the first round. There are triumphs and defeats; people recall the sweet moments but you have to remember everything that happened.'

Porta had seven shots at beating New Zealand and, until Argentina finally managed to defeat the All Blacks in a full Test match at the 30th attempt in 2020, had played a key role in their best result, the 21–21 draw in Buenos Aires in 1985.

'My first trip to New Zealand was with the Pumas in 1979. That team arrived in Auckland on the same weekend France were leaving having drawn their Test series 1–1 with the All Blacks and no one knew us. So people would tell us that if we won one match of all those we were going to play on the tour we could consider it a success.

'Most of us were young, lots of university students; many of us didn't speak English and gradually the team took shape and we won the first six matches of the tour and reached the first Test unbeaten having gained incredible popularity in the islands.'

Argentina had already played New Zealand at home in 1976 but the internationals in that series and in 1979 were capped Tests only for the Pumas. When the All Blacks returned to Argentina in 1985 they too regarded the two matches as fully fledged Tests.

'So, that was the start of a link I had with New Zealand that lasted many years because I went there several times invited to play, as part of the South African Barbarians. Also on a tour that was made at Easter with a mixed team of veteran All Blacks mixed with young players starting out as All Blacks and some foreign players and that gave me the chance to have very close links with New Zealand players.

'Of course when you play rugby you know the most traditional teams like England or New Zealand are those you always want to beat and I think we saw the progress of Argentine rugby in that victory the Pumas had a short time ago over the All Blacks which really was something very emotional.'

Porta played alongside some exceptional backs in his early years in the Pumas, then led a side with a magnificent pack, beating Australia and France and drawing with England and New Zealand.

'Argentina is a place where, thanks to the work put in at the clubs which are totally amateur and the people give their time freely, there is a constant flow of talent coming through.

'We've had players of the quality of Martín Sansot, Juan Hernández, also lots who today are playing abroad. Argentina will always produce good players. I mentioned Sansot for the ease with which he played, for his skills. Then there are players who are symbols, like Pochola Silva who was a source of inspiration for many young players of my age, and others like Luis Gradín, Arturo Rodríguez Jurado, Alejandro Travaglini.

'My involvement today is as president of my club where I see my role as trying to ensure boys playing in my club have the same opportunities I had because I see the game as something important in young people's lives but also fleeting. What's important in rugby is what you learn on the field, the friends you make and the values you learn and then apply in life.

'One of the competitive advantages Argentine players have over players of other countries is their origins and development. They are all born in the clubs where rugby is totally amateur, where you always want to play even when you're injured and it's that amateur spirit that sets Argentine players apart and I'm sure they will always have a place in any team, professional or not.'

ELEVEN

GAZELLE

———————————— 🐆 ————————————

RUGBY IN ARGENTINA, within its largely middle-class confines, is very mixed in terms of the origin of the players.

There was the British influence first, founding clubs and schools, but during and after the boom in immigration in the 19th and early 20th centuries people from many different European nations sought out these clubs and sent their children to such schools.

Martín Sansot, the player Hugo Porta said was the best he had ever seen, was extremely gifted as a young man who could have dedicated himself to any sport and who played a lot of football outside the rugby season.

He was also a good rider, learning bareback at his father's 'campo' (ranch) in Córdoba province in the centre of the country, 600 kilometres from Buenos Aires.

Rugby was available to him through his school, the Anglo-Argentine St John's School in the northern suburbs of Buenos Aires, which used the playing fields at different times of rugby clubs Pueyrredón and BACRC for their sports activities, not having fields of their own.

The family home was close to Pueyrredón, who had a team in

the Buenos Aires first division championship in which Sansot played at full back for 12 years from 1974 to 1985, and opened his path to the Pumas.

He impressed the media and crowds on Pumas tours of Wales in 1976 and England in 1978 and was described as a gazelle. He was slight, never weighing more than 70 kilos, but fast, brave and elusive.

He regularly joined the three-quarters in attack like the time he laid on Argentina's first try in Wales's last-gasp 20–19 win over the Pumas at Cardiff Arms Park in 1976.

The number of British names in Argentine representative sides in the first half of the 20th century dwindled, their places taken by such as Sansot, whose father had French Basque heritage and his mother mixed Spanish and Scottish origins. His uncle Jorge played for Club Universitario de Buenos Aires (CUBA) and once for Argentina against the Oxford and Cambridge touring side in 1948.

The first time Sansot played for Argentina was the opening match of their first tour of France in 1975 against a Côte Basque selection in Bayonne when he was 20.

'We are on our way to the match in a coach when I suddenly see through the window a veterinary shop called Sansot. And I was a veterinary student at the time.

'The elitist label attached to rugby in Argentina maybe had to do with having to pay to play rugby, which wasn't the case with football. Access to rugby was limited but at the same time clubs would help those who really wanted to play but couldn't afford to.

'There were people who couldn't pay the monthly membership fee, or didn't have the gear or couldn't pay for the trips so the rest of the team would cover that kid's costs and he'd become our friend because we'd all see each other on Tuesdays, Thursdays and Saturdays for practice and games.

'Rugby became popular thanks to the Pumas, from 1999, the first World Cup in which they managed to get past the qualifying phase, so from then on we started to make some noise in Argentina and the world. Then from 2007 we were no longer the black sheep of rugby.

'I was kind of unusual in my development as a rugby player. I was never a rugby fanatic; it was never the central thing in my life. I was a sports fanatic in general: rugby, football, tennis, squash – I loved them because they were intense.

'And I was always self-taught. I never had anyone who told me how to improve some facet of my game.

'I had a very free background, having spent a lot of time in the 'campo'. We kids did all kinds of things and my dad said, "Here you come to work; if you want to mess about you can stay in Buenos Aires" and we'd go because of the freedom; we had a 5,000-hectare (12,000 acres) "garden" – you could choose the tractor or the horse and I always chose the horse. I was around eight, ten and my dad would say, "No saddle; you can have that when you've learnt to ride like the Indians." We'd work from dawn to dusk.

'And that gave me a sports grounding, because it gives you lateral vision. You've got to have your antennae turned on all the time; you know where to run, look for space, you have a very wide vision and I believe I had that facility that maybe people in the city didn't have: peripheral vision.

'The only mentor I had was a coach who talked about attitude, Angel 'Papuchi' Guastella, who would always say: "Look, lads. All that interests me is that when the match ends I have to go and get you from the field and not see you walking off because if you walk off it means you have energy that you didn't leave on the field . . . You have to give your all."'

Guastella was the former Pueyrredón and Argentina fly-half who coached the original 1965 Pumas and had another spell in charge of Argentina in 1978 when his team, including Sansot and Porta, drew with England at Twickenham.

Sansot had won half of his 18 caps between 1975 and 1978 before dislocating his right shoulder during a first division match for Pueyrredón against CASI in 1979 when he was 24.

He put his shoulder out half a dozen times, the next on tour with the Pumas in New Zealand that September but played in both Tests and also in the drawn home series against Australia in October 1979 before having an operation and a harness made to be able to continue playing.

'I had no problem with frontal tackles but tackling wide I did . . . I had limited movement because I couldn't raise my arm but I'd find a way and I had other qualities. My defence wasn't quite so strong or impressive but I still got by.'

It is likely Sansot would have had a more intense Pumas career and higher profile outside Argentina, possibly on a par with Porta, with a perfectly good shoulder. He played another five Tests, the last two for South America XV against the Springboks in South Africa in 1984, before retiring aged 31.

TWELVE

'LOS DESAPARECIDOS'

DURING THE DARK, violent period in Argentine history of the late 1970s and early '80s when the country was governed by a brutal military regime, 20 players from a single rugby club were among the thousands of 'desaparecidos' – kidnapped, tortured and murdered because of their political beliefs.

They were victims of a far-right purge of mainly young left-wingers by clandestine gangs of paramilitary thugs that started during the final years of the civilian Peronist government and became a state-sanctioned genocide by the military dictatorship that took charge in a 1976 coup.

Many of the players of La Plata Rugby Club were National University of La Plata (UNLP) students with a strong social conscience and commitment to helping forge a better society and whose values rhymed with those of the sport they loved: altruism, solidarity, loyalty and friendship.

Peronism, the country's biggest political movement that was ousted from power and banned from activity in 1955 when a military coup deposed President Juan Domingo Perón, had developed into a hydra of factions with far right and left at the extremes.

The young, fed up with the musical chairs of military and civilian governments that followed, were excited about the possibilities of a new and better country when Perón was allowed to return in 1973 from 18 years in exile and run for president again.

Perón died in 1974 and his widow Isabel, the vice-president, took office. But there was a heavy presence of the right in the government, led by the nefarious Minister of Social Welfare (and Perón's former secretary in exile), José López Rega, who created the Triple A (Argentine Anticommunist Alliance), targeting left-wingers and anyone they suspected of being associated with them and making them disappear.

The military, determined to wipe out even the slightest hint of socialism, organised the practice of arresting suspected dissidents, actually kidnapping them, giving them no trial, torturing and then 'disappearing' them, many weighted down and thrown from planes into the Río de la Plata (River Plate).

This was the fate of tens of thousands, among them 20 young men between the ages of 20 and 31 who had played for La Plata RC before disappearing between 1975 and 1978. They were among more than 150 known rugby players, by a long way the sport most affected, who were identified as victims during this terrible chapter in Argentine history.

A couple of these players could have gone on to enjoy international careers, according to former teammates, coaches and La Plata fans.

La Plata, capital of Buenos Aires province, is a quiet university city of about 900,000 inhabitants 50 kilometres from Argentina's sprawling 10-million capital, Buenos Aires.

Unlike other Argentine cities, its streets are identified by numbers rather than names and it is known for its particular grid with green spaces every six blocks and diagonal roads criss-crossing the main urban area.

In sporting terms it is best known for its two biggest football teams, four-time South American champions Estudiantes and Gimnasia y Esgrima LP.

La Plata RC's two main city rivals are Los Tilos and San Luis, both of which produced former Pumas captains, Héctor Silva of Los Tilos in the 1960s and San Luis's Agustín Creevy in the second decade of this century.

The All Blacks played Argentina three times in the city at the modern Ciudad de la Plata stadium, also known as Estadio Único, in Rugby Championship matches in 2012, 2013 and 2014.

Walking the streets of the city, it is hard to imagine how dangerous they became for young students at the UNLP, its main university, as left-wing militants got caught up in the violence that engulfed Argentina in the 1970s.

One of that generation of players, Raúl Barandiarán, said: 'During those years there was a lot of political effervescence; militancy was quite normal. We all came from state schools or studied at the UNLP and also felt a lot of solidarity [for each other] . . . [And] La Plata was a different club where freedoms were taken to an extreme.'

La Plata RC differed from the norm in rugby in Argentina at the time, which was a minority upper-middle-class sport, considered elitist by critics.

'In 1973, for instance, we players went on strike because [the club authorities] wanted to impose on us a coach we didn't want . . . That was unprecedented; nothing like that had ever happened anywhere,' Barandiarán recounted in the book *Maten al Rugbier* (Kill the Rugby Player), in which journalist Claudio Gómez tells the story of the 20 who disappeared.

La Plata RC started as a rugby branch at Gimnasia y Esgrima in 1925 before they were banned by the River Plate Rugby Union, predecessor to the UAR, when the round-ball game became professional in 1931.

Out on their own, the rugby players began their own club at new premises and, lacking the funds to buy a complete new set of shirts, they dyed the football colours of white with a horizontal blue band round the middle a deep yellow several times to hide the blue and earned the nickname Canaries from the English language *Buenos Aires Herald* newspaper.

They reached the Buenos Aires top division in 1953 and won their only URBA title in 1995. They won the defunct National Club Championship, in which teams from all the country's unions took part, in 2007.

Some of the disappeared players had already helped La Plata make a name for themselves by winning Buenos Aires province seven-a-side competitions in 1973 and 1974.

That side had a strong influence on the sevens game in Argentina and might have been the core of a great XV but for the fate of their players.

Another member of that generation is Gonzalo 'Nicha' Albarracín, who coached the 1995 champions and later became Argentina's Sevens coach when the country hosted the 2001 Sevens World Cup in Mar del Plata, the Atlantic seaside resort 400 kilometres south of Buenos Aires.

There, his side, including Agustín Pichot, Felipe Contepomi and Ignacio Corleto, reached the semi-finals before losing to Jonah Lomu's New Zealand, who won the title.

The first La Plata RC victim of state terrorism was Hernán Rocca, a 21-year-old medical student who had played as scrum-half and captain and been called up to the Pumitas, the under-20 national side, but had become militant with a left-wing organisation that worked among the poor.

He was kidnapped outside his family's home one night and found the next day with 21 bullet wounds in his back, blindfolded and with his hands tied.

His brother Marcelo had been involved in the left-wing ERP (People's Revolutionary Army) guerrilla group and although he had left it, he believed Hernán's murder might either have been a mistake and right-wing paramilitaries were after him or a warning. He fled into exile in Spain.

One of Barandiarán's friends was Santiago Sánchez Viamonte, an architecture student nicknamed 'El Chueco' (bandy legs) who was 'disappeared' in 1977. Having made his first division debut at 17, he was a versatile back who played mainly at fly-half and is widely regarded as the best La Plata RC player. An emerging talent, it was often said at the club that he 'could be as good as El Chueco'.

Sánchez Viamonte played for La Plata for seven years before prioritising his political convictions.

Barandiarán, like others who survived when they could have been victims, said it took him many years of therapy to try to get over the loss of friends and teammates.

He tells the story of how, in 1974, some of his teammates joined him at his parents' summer home at the seaside in San Bernardo for some training ahead of the Mar del Plata sevens further down the coast.

He and his close friend Otilio were on the beach when another three including Santiago Sánchez Viamonte came from a hazy distance walking along the sand towards them carrying their bags.

'That image was stamped so strongly in my mind that until the mid-90s when my father died I'd go to San Bernardo every summer and whenever I went to the beach I'd look southwards hoping to see them coming back in the distance carrying their bags,' Barandiarán said.

'More than 20 years had gone by and I was still hoping. I could never, ever get over that feeling.'

Like him, the families of the disappeared clung to the hope they might reappear one day, not least the mother of La Plata RC's Rodolfo Axat who kept paying her son's monthly club membership until her death in 2002.

Many relatives became militant in the search for the disappeared. Mothers formed the Madres de Plaza de Mayo group, who paraded every Thursday from 1977 at the square of that name in front of the Casa Rosada (pink Government House) in Buenos Aires demanding from the authorities information about the whereabouts of their children.

Some disappeared women were kidnapped along with their small children or were pregnant and gave birth in captivity, which led to a parallel group, the Abuelas (grandmothers) de Plaza de Mayo.

Following the demise of the military regime after their ill-fated invasion of the Malvinas islands and defeat in the Falklands War against Britain, it was the bravery of these women and the actions of human rights organisations that kept up the pressure on the democratically elected governments after 1983 to bring so many of the perpetrators of the genocide to justice.

Marcelo Bettini, a 21-year-old law student who played for La Plata RC between the ages of 13 and 18, killed himself in November 1976 swallowing a cyanide pill when he was captured in a raid. He had told his best friend he had the pill on him at all times in case he got caught. 'I'm not going to let those bastards torture me,' he said.

His family didn't know what had happened to him and what followed, as his 60-year-old father Antonio, an eminent public prosecutor and university lecturer, sought news of his whereabouts, turned into a family tragedy.

Marcelo Bettini's father and 29-year-old brother-in-law Jorge Devoto, a former Argentine naval officer with good military connections, both disappeared during their search for news of Marcelo and then even his 77-year-old grandmother, a member of one of La Plata city's wealthiest and most traditional families, with the perpetrators ransacking and then stealing her home and assets.

It took more than 30 years for the chief culprit, Buenos Aires province police chief Miguel Etchecolatz, who argued at his trial that he 'had only killed terrorists', to finally be brought to justice. He was sentenced to consecutive life terms in prison for homicide, torture and kidnapping.

THIRTEEN

PUCCIO

THE RETURN OF democracy with an elected civilian government in 1983 left in limbo hundreds, even thousands of paramilitary personnel who had helped the dictatorship wage its Dirty War against opponents since 1976.

One such man was Arquímedes Puccio, an apparently respectable resident of San Isidro, a lawyer and accountant who had worked in the diplomatic corps as a young man, but whose chequered background included links with the secret police, the Triple A (Argentine Anticommunist Alliance) and other illegal activities.

He was alleged to have helped kidnap businessman Segismundo Pels in a 1973 operation led by the infamous Etchecolatz.

Puccio led a small gang of men who kidnapped and murdered wealthy business people between 1982 and 1985. The first three victims were men, two in their twenties, one soon to be married, the other recently married. The third, married with two small daughters, was in his thirties.

'The Puccio clan inaugurated the era of kidnappings post dictatorship,' wrote journalist Rodolfo Palacios in his book *El Clan Puccio*, published in 2015. A film was also made called *El Clan* and a TV series.

Puccio had a list of other potential victims but only managed to kidnap one more, Nélida Bollini de Prado, a wealthy 58-year-old woman who was rescued alive from a cellar where she had been held for a month when police raided the Puccio home after capturing Arquímedes as he was about to pick up a ransom payment in the city.

One of the members of the gang was Puccio's eldest son Alejandro, a wing three-quarters who played for CASI – the club located a mere 200 metres from the family home where three of the four victims had been held – helping them win three Buenos Aires titles in the 1980s. He won three Pumas caps and also played twice for South America XV.

The first victim, Ricardo Manoukian, was heir to a supermarket chain in the northern suburbs of Buenos Aires where San Isidro is located and a keen rugby player.

He and Alejandro Puccio were not chums, but they knew each other and Manoukian admired the winger's style. Their respective girlfriends were friends and the couples had been at a party on Manoukian's boat in the Uruguayan resort of Punta del Este, according to the victim's brother Guillermo, who was convinced Alejandro was involved in the crimes.

Alejandro Puccio was alleged to have played a part in Manoukian's kidnapping by stopping him in his car to say hello as if he was there by chance on a San Isidro avenue. The gang swooped, bundling him into a van and driving him to the Puccio residence.

He was also alleged to have opened the gates to the Puccio residence when the second victim, engineer Eduardo Aulet, was driven in by gang members hidden in a car some months later.

Aulet played rugby and football. He was a very good striker who was offered a trial at Boca Juniors when he was in his teens but turned it down to concentrate on his studies.

Ricardo Manoukian and Eduardo Aulet's families did not go to the police after Arquímedes Puccio had told them not to, but rather than being released on payment of the ransom money the victims were driven to remote areas out of town and executed.

The third victim, Emilio Naum, resisted the gang's attempt to kidnap him and was shot dead in a struggle, while Bollini's family did go to the police.

Arquímedes Puccio was a verbose, boastful, manipulative man who said in one interview he had nothing to do with the crimes attributed to him, then in another that he was Argentina's greatest criminal mastermind.

He managed to get other members of the gang to pull the trigger on their victims, citing loyalty to the cause they had all sealed with their blood.

Alejandro Puccio denied having been a part of the gang and said he had simply suffered the fate of being a psychopath's son, but other members claimed he had played a part and he, like his father and three others, were sentenced to life in prison.

He survived four attempts at suicide, including in 1987 when he leapt from the fifth floor of a stairwell at the Buenos Aires law courts but landed on the corrugated metal roof of a kiosk rather than the tiled ground floor, causing such a loud bang that people in the hall took it for a bomb.

Soon after his release, in 2008, he died of pneumonia aged 49 – only two months after his father left prison – having served nearly 24 years. Arquímedes was 83 when he died, in 2013.

Alejandro Puccio was 21 when he won his three Argentina caps in the 1979 South American Championship with victories against Chile, Paraguay and Brazil. He toured South Africa with Hugo Porta's South American Jaguars in 1982 and played for the team that shared the series against the Springboks after winning the second Test.

His friends and teammates at CASI, where Alejandro had played since the age of seven and was well liked and admired, refused at first to believe he had had any part in his father's crimes.

The gang's arrests, including Alejandro's, were less than a week before CASI won the title in August 1985 and because he was missing from the team in their last match of the season at home they did not celebrate with the traditional run around the pitch saluting their fans.

Some went to visit him in prison to lend their support and two CASI members who were attorneys took charge of his defence.

It was a huge blow to the club that Alejandro should have been involved in kidnapping and murder and they struggled with their disappointment and feelings of betrayal when the truth came out.

Former CASI and Pumas lock Eliseo Branca, who along with the rest of the club had believed Alejandro Puccio innocent, was horrified to learn his teammate had been involved in the crimes and to discover he was on a list of names drawn up by Arquímedes as a future victim of his gang.

'I was on the list. I found out from a friend who was the owner of Banco de Italia, who knew him (Alejandro) through me. I was standing up for him and he says: "What, you're defending him? But you're on the list."'

CASI took years to get over the Puccio case and did not allow their premises to be used for the film or TV series.

Arquímedes Puccio took the military regime's practice of kidnapping people and appropriating their belongings, including their children (some born in captivity), and applied it to a private money-making scheme, says Miguel García Lombardi, a sports psychologist with close links to rugby.

'He had a psychopathic control over his family, who must have all known to some degree what he was doing.

'In the 1980s, your father's voice was the law. It was very difficult to be against your father. His brother left home but Alejandro stayed. He continued to play rugby and hang out with his friends, while at the same time he was bound by his father's diktats.

'There's a very powerful denial mechanism in which Alejandro tells himself, "I am a rugby player, I have a girlfriend, I'm from the well-heeled, upper middle class and to hold that up I need to kidnap."

'He lunges over the balcony at the law courts to [try to] kill himself at the very moment his friends go there to tell him they support him and that's when he can't dissociate one life from the other and once they merge the pain is too hard to bear.'

FOURTEEN

'THIRD HALF'

IMAGINE FOR A moment that an England prop called John Smith was playing his club rugby in France, the Rugby Football Union had decided the coach could pick players wherever they were based and the agreement was that the player would join the team at London's Heathrow airport for the start of a tour of a country in the southern hemisphere.

Smith gets to Heathrow and gradually squad members appear and say hello, but they are shuffling their feet and not saying much, perhaps a little too embarrassed to tell him there is something wrong.

The unthinkable had happened . . . he hadn't been told he had been dropped.

Omar Hasan was the victim of an episode in November 1997 as the nearly forgotten man of Argentina's Latin Cup squad – only to end up playing in all three matches.

Hasan, who had been playing for the Lions in Wellington in New Zealand's NPC (National Provincial Championship), was to meet up with the Pumas squad in Buenos Aires to fly on to France for the four-nation tournament that also included Italy and Romania.

'I had agreed to go to the south of France to play in the Latin Cup, so I arrived at Ezeiza airport expecting to meet up with the others there.

'But in the meantime I hadn't had any communication with anyone at the UAR and presumably [coach] José Luis Imhoff had changed his mind – I've no idea for what reason – and no one had told me. Gradually the guys were arriving but none dared tell me at first that I wasn't on the list.'

Hasan laughs about it now but he was not laughing when he found out he was apparently surplus to requirements.

'It was all a bit confusing and I was fuming but Imhoff, when he saw me, came over smiling, opened his arms for an embrace and said warmly: "Hello, Omarcito, how are you?" And of course a director came over to explain what was going on.

'"Are you prepared to come with us now?" Imhoff asked, as if he knew nothing about it. Obviously I really wanted to go . . . "Yes, of course," I said.'

Hasan had just flown from New Zealand to Argentina and was about to take another long flight to France, 30 hours in the air all told. A ticket was bought for him but there was no more room in business class so it was tourist class for him.

'I was really tired and needed to rest. Someone did offer to change places but I turned him down.'

The Pumas players had only four months previously secured better travelling conditions from the UAR when they toured New Zealand that June.

Imhoff may have not had anything to do with Hasan's omission from the squad. The UAR was in a state of flux in those days with some officials in high places very much against professionals playing for the Pumas.

UAR president Luis Gradín and coach Imhoff were not among them and had welcomed two other front-row professionals, Federico Méndez and Mauricio Reggiardo, back for Tests against South Africa and England in 1996. Méndez was then with Natal and Reggiardo had joined Castres.

By the time of the Latin Cup in October 1997, Pichot and Rolando Martin were with Richmond, captain Lisandro Arbizu was at Brive, lock Germán Llanes was on the point of joining Bath, wing Diego Giannantonio was at Piacenza and centre Fabián Turnes had returned home from nearly a decade as an exile in Italy.

Argentina finished the tournament, the second and last of its kind, in second place behind France after beating Romania 45–18, drawing 18–18 with Italy and losing 32–27 to the hosts.

By then Hasan had also acquired a reputation for his fine baritone voice, often singing in front of teammates and opponents at post-match dinners or booze-ups that Argentines call *el tercer tiempo*, an integral part of amateur rugby culture (see Glossary and the CASI–SIC chapter).

Hasan took advantage of a piano and someone who could play to sing some of his favourite Neapolitan songs in the lobby of the team's hotel in Lourdes one morning after practice at the Latin Cup and a small crowd of Italian tourists gathered to enjoy the informal show.

'It happened all the time. One of my best memories was after a match we played against England at Twickenham, during a very formal dinner. Someone said, "Hey, Omar; sing something." So I got up on the stage and the English, just imagine with all the protocol, they went wild.

'One of the English players also climbed up and sang, and their team doctor too. It developed into a real '*tercer tiempo*' which had been disappearing due to professionalism.

'A team official came and thanked me. He said I'd created a real post-match spirit.'

Professional rugby seems to have virtually killed off the post-match fraternity enjoyed by amateurs but Argentine players have always tried to maintain it, loyal to their amateur spirit despite playing professionally.

Hasan has pursued a career as a singer and variety artist, including opera and tango shows, since he retired from rugby aged 37 in 2008 and remained living in the south of France.

He had a long and successful rugby career with 64 caps as a tight-head prop, starting at the Natación y Gimnasia (swimming and gymnastics) club in Tucumán, one of Argentina's strongest provincial unions in the north-west of the country.

As a teenager, the chances were slim of being spotted for a place in the national age-group Pumitas (little Pumas) teams that took part in junior world championships.

'I was never able to play for the Pumitas because of the way Argentine rugby was organised before. If you weren't a first-choice player in your provincial team, as an 18-year-old no one got to see you. You got no chances, above all if you were from the interior [of the country]. There was no one following all the players.

'That was one of the big disadvantages for rugby in the interior. The game, and everything else in Argentina for that matter, was very much centred in Buenos Aires. And very quickly you became too old for the Pumitas.'

But Hasan got his chance when he was picked for the Argentine team to take part in the 1992 Student World Cup in Italy when he was 21.

'The team was thrown together at the last minute but with some very good players who would later become Pumas – several from Tucumán, Rosario, Mendoza, Córdoba – and we gave the Pumas of that time a hiding in a practice.

'Our first group match was against South Africa. The country was just emerging from its ban for apartheid. They were giants but we beat them, and we punished them in the scrum.

'Next up was England. They had prepared a whole strategy based on facing a right-handed fly-half but we also had a left-hander, 'Chacho' Herrera, and he played and on top of that in the scrum we gave them a good hiding.

'We lost to the All Blacks in the semi-finals and finished third. The last of those tournaments was played in 1996. Those kinds of tournaments were discontinued with professionalism; they disappeared.'

By 1992, Hasan had made it into the Pumas squad for the tour of Europe and played in midweek games. He then had to wait until 1995 to win his first cap, in a South American Championship Test against Uruguay, but he missed out on that year's World Cup in South Africa.

Hasan's early professional years involved some globetrotting, first making the leap from Tucumán to Wellington to play for the Lions after getting an offer during the June 1997 tour of New Zealand with the Pumas. It was a brief stay before rejoining the Pumas for the Latin Cup that October.

He had kept in touch with fellow prop Pato Noriega, who had joined the ACT Brumbies in 1996 when the Super 12 was created. Noriega told him the Brumbies were looking for a replacement for Ewen McKenzie who was injured . . . so it was next stop Australia.

'It was a dream to play in the Super 12. I went for one season and was coached by Eddie Jones, who was very pleased and would have liked me to stay on for a second season but I couldn't because of Australian union rules limiting foreign players to favour potential Wallabies, especially in a pre-World Cup year.

'I was at three different clubs in a year. I joined Brumbies in December 1997 and left in August 1998, went back to Wellington for another NPC and then was in France at the end of that year.'

Touring with Argentina that November, which included a Test against France in Nantes, Hasan was offered a place as a medical 'joker' covering for an injured prop at small French club Auch by former France captain and coach Jacques Fouroux, who was their president.

'That gave me six months in France to prepare for the 1999 World Cup and then see what happened next; maybe get in contact with a bigger club. Auch were semi-professional.

'A month after going to Auch I was contacted by Agen, a much bigger club in all respects. I joined them after the World

Cup and we reached the 2002 Top 16 final but lost to Biarritz by a drop goal in the final seconds.'

Hasan had settled in the south of France, working on his other passion, singing, and after the 2003 World Cup in Australia he joined Toulouse, so he was one of a large number of Pumas resident in the country when he played in his third World Cup there in 2007.

With Toulouse, he won the Heineken Cup in 2005 with victory in the final against the Stade Français side of his Pumas colleagues Pichot, Rodrigo Roncero and Juan Martín Hernández.

He closed out his rugby career with a Top 14 title, Toulouse beating Mario Ledesma's Clermont in the 2008 final.

FIFTEEN

YOUNGEST CAPTAIN

'There were many, many defeats but that meant
we enjoyed the victories all the more.'
Lisandro Arbizu

LISANDRO ARBIZU, WHO succeeded the great Hugo Porta as Argentina's fly-half, is well remembered for his skills and perseverance as a member of a generation of Pumas caught up in Argentina's fraught relationship with the advent of professional rugby in the 1990s.

Named captain at 21 in 1992 – the youngest player ever to lead the Pumas – Arbizu was one of the first Argentines to play professionally abroad and was Brive's fly-half in the European Cup final against Bath in 1997.

Arbizu won 86 Argentina caps after making his debut at 18 in 1990, captained the Pumas 48 times, a record broken by Agustín Creevy in 2018, played at three World Cups and missed out on a fourth through injury in 2003, retiring from international rugby in 2005.

Yet his long career was marked mainly by adversity during a transitional decade for the Pumas in which they failed to get past the pool phase at the first three World Cups and drew on their bountiful reserves of passion to finally breach the barrier in 1999.

Arbizu's progress from his club Belgrano Athletic in the URBA first division to the Pumas via the Buenos Aires representative side and under-20 Pumitas was meteoric.

He helped Buenos Aires beat England 26–23 in the opening match of their tour in June 1990 in which Argentina shared the Test series 1–1.

He made his Pumas debut as a replacement in a 20–18 defeat by Ireland in Dublin on a tour of the British Isles at the end of that year. Argentina were led by Porta, who had retired in 1987 but came back for the tour to help blood a raft of raw newcomers.

'It was a very long tour, 40 days, with a mix of very young players who were starting out and others with lots of experience,' Arbizu said. 'World rugby was growing apace and Argentina were getting bogged down.'

Arbizu did not play in the crushing 51–0 defeat by Will Carling's England at Twickenham, when Federico Méndez was famously sent off for punching Paul Ackford.

Porta was injured during the first half of the next Test against Scotland and Arbizu took his place in a 49–3 loss at Murrayfield.

'The period in which I started was mainly about defence – there was a big difference between defence and attack [in the Pumas team].

'I loved creating and leading both as a fly-half and centre but I had to develop the defensive part of my game a bit out of survival.

'When I started playing [for the Pumas], their strength lay in the forwards. We three-quarters were opportunists,' he said. 'Professionalism was growing fast and you could see [in our opponents] the difference in organisation, structure, dedication to prepare for international matches.

'My career was full of adversity because it was a period of transition from the great team of the 1980s to a renewal of players. There were many, many defeats but that meant we enjoyed the victories all the more.'

There was one such win during his first tour as captain in 1992 when a run of nine defeats in Tests against major rugby nations was ended by a totally unexpected 24–20 victory over France in Nantes, Argentina's first away win over the French.

Arbizu was part of six successive defeats at the 1991 and 1995 World Cups, including a 24-18 loss to England in Durban, when Argentina won the try count two-nil, with Arbizu scoring one.

After winning a home series 2–0 against Scotland in 1994, Argentina lost 12 successive Tests against the top teams, punctuated by wins over the likes of Italy, Canada, the United States and Romania, until they shared another home series with England winning the second Test 31–13 in 1997.

However, given no time for a break, the Pumas flew to New Zealand where they suffered their worst ever defeat, 93–8 in the first Test and lost the second 62–10 which highlighted the gulf that separated the teams in the 1990s.

The players, however, grew stronger as the 1999 World Cup approached and Arbizu was to lead them to their World Cup breakthrough, hardened by a coaching crisis in the build-up when Héctor Méndez resigned over differences with the UAR after a warm-up tour of Scotland and Ireland.

Former All Blacks coach Alex 'Grizz' Wyllie had been assisting the team as a consultant but had gone home to New Zealand on personal business and was not expected back until the tournament. He found out while he was away that he had been left in sole charge.

'It was a moment of maturity for the team when we found ourselves orphaned, without a coach,' Arbizu said. 'While we waited for Wyllie we made ourselves strong. It was a challenge to play that World Cup digging deep into ourselves.

'Our strength at the time lay in our great defence, a great pack of forwards and great teamwork, and then the opportunism of individual players.

'Wyllie imposed on us his discipline and culture as a great player and coach with simple but vital instructions. He took the fortitude of the team and worked on the forwards' scrummaging, lineout and defence. And we as players took it on ourselves to break the mould.'

SIXTEEN

WORLD CUP

A SHOCK 28–9 defeat by Fiji in Argentina's first ever World Cup match helped set in motion a period of underachievement in the game's showpiece event lasting more than a decade.

The Pumas, having been seeded behind the All Blacks in Pool 3 of the inaugural tournament hosted by New Zealand and Australia in 1987, had hoped and planned to progress into the quarter-finals.

It would never have been expected for Argentina to punch higher than their standing outside Europe's top five nations and the two southern hemisphere giants (South Africa were banned because of their apartheid policy) but that seeding meant they should have taken the eighth quarter-final berth.

Argentina had enjoyed an impressive set of results against the leading nations in the previous decade following the near miss in a 20–19 loss to Wales in 1976.

The Pumas had draws with two England teams, a draw and a win against France, two wins over Australia, a draw against New Zealand and a Hugo Porta-inspired dismantling of South Africa., with Argentina disguised as a South America XV.

The balance of the World Cup squad picked by coaches Héctor

Silva and Angel Guastella and captained by the great Porta in his twilight years was rather heavily inclined towards youth with not enough depth of experience.

The 35-year-old Porta was uncharacteristically off his kicking early on against Fiji when Argentina could have built a good lead, surprisingly accepting sand provided to make a little mound for the ball at his place kicks which he had never done before and missing three penalties.

'I still ask myself why I took the sand because I had never kicked using it,' Porta said many years later. 'That shows how bad everything in the team was.'

The Fijians worked their way into the match, losing their respect for their opponents, and gradually made inroads via their wonderful handling skills in attack to run in four tries to one penalty try for the Pumas and five points kicked by Porta.

The Argentines beat Italy 25–16 and saved their few best moves for the hardest rivals, losing 46–15 to New Zealand, scoring one of only four tries the All Blacks conceded in the tournament.

New Zealand, who beat France in the final, had run at least 70 points each past Fiji and Italy who both finished level on two points with Argentina, the islanders going through on tries scored.

Rodolfo 'Michingo' O'Reilly, who had been in charge of South America XV on their second tour of South Africa in 1982 when they shared the series 1–1 with the Springboks, took charge of the Pumas for most of the second World Cup cycle.

But O'Reilly was sacked in 1991 after the Pumas lost two World Cup qualifiers against Canada, away and home, which put them in a tough Pool 3 for the tournament hosted by the countries that played in Europe's Five Nations Championship.

He was replaced by Luis Gradín, a member of the 'original' 1965 Pumas, in itself not a bad change of coach, but it went against the grain of continuity.

Argentina lost 32–19 to Australia, the eventual champions, 16–7 to Wales and 35–12 to Western Samoa in the first of three meetings with the South Sea Islanders at consecutive World Cups.

Argentina went into a slump that lasted most of the decade.

The rare high points in the years before the third World Cup were a first away victory over France in Nantes in 1992, which was a huge upset under coaches Gradín and José Luis Imhoff, and a home series win against Scotland in 1994 with new coach Héctor 'Pipo' Méndez in charge.

There was controversy in the final minutes of the deciding second Test against the Scots at Ferro Carril Oeste when Argentina had 16 men on the field with Leandro Bouza slipping on while Guillermo del Castillo lay injured and getting treatment without prior assent from the touch judge.

Bouza was on for at least 23 seconds and some reports said longer with del Castillo already recovered and the Scots complaining about the manner in which it happened as Argentina hung on for a 19–17 victory, having won the first Test 16–15.

Pipo Méndez didn't get to the 1995 World Cup in South Africa, being replaced by Alejandro Petra after his success with Tucumán, who under his guidance had won the Argentine provincial championship seven times between 1985 and 1993.

Petra may be best remembered as the man who took Agustín Pichot in his squad but did not give him a minute's action despite the livewire 20-year-old scrum-half's growing reputation and legion of fans back home.

The Pumas scored two tries to none against England in their Pool B opener in Durban but lost 24–18 thanks to the kicking of Rob Andrew that punished Argentine penalties.

The first try was scored by prop Pato Noriega in a move the Argentines called 'La Gran Cacho', named after teammate Marcelo 'Cacho' Urbano, a prop and like Pichot a squad member who saw no action at the tournament.

From a five-metre tap penalty, the whole pack charged England's defensive line and bundled Noriega over. The move was banned by the International Rugby Board (IRB) before Argentina's next game.

Argentina then moved to East London where they next lost 32–26 to old foes Western Samoa.

In their last match, they lost 31–25 to Italy despite winning the try count, a defeat masterminded by Diego Domínguez, who might have been playing for Argentina, the country of his birth, if he had been encouraged more to become Porta's successor, instead seeking more international action in Europe and being banned from all rugby in Argentina.

Professional era

PROFESSIONALISM BECAME OPEN after that World Cup and the gulf between the best teams and Argentina was highlighted on a tour of New Zealand in 1997 where Argentina fell to their worst ever defeat, 93–8 to the All Blacks.

On the one hand, the Pumas travelled in business class for the first time, a new gain on the slow march towards professional conditions for the team even though the players were amateur. On the other, they embarked on the long journey to New Zealand less than 24 hours after the second Test of a home series against England (that they drew 1–1), without getting a break.

The second Test against the All Blacks was only marginally better, losing 62–10, and they went on to share a home series with Australia at the end of the year but they badly needed to get more wins under their belts.

Instead, the Pumas entered the next World Cup year on the back of three Test defeats on tour in Europe in November 1998 with growing feelings against coach Imhoff among senior players.

There was one constant during this troublesome 1999 World Cup cycle: Wyllie, who came on board as the Pumas' first foreign coach to help steer them towards better times.

Gradín, who became UAR president in 1996 for a four-year term, reached out to Wyllie when the New Zealander was coaching Eastern Province in South Africa.

'It was a very tough time for Argentine rugby,' Gradín says. 'The professional era did not come as such a surprise in the rest of the world, but it was here. Although we knew about it, no one in Argentina earned any money, not even the coaches.

'When the IRB decided on the big changes, they put us in a huge quandary. Either we went into isolation or we went ahead with the changes, which is when the UAR stepped in, trying not to lose our club rugby which was and is absolutely amateur.

'We sought to keep our local rugby as it had always been and get up to date with international rugby. It was a violent change for everyone: we had crises, advances and setbacks, but in the end we all found our way. I was very close to it all, getting some things wrong and others right.

'Alex was very important in this transition; he helped us a lot to become professional, quite apart from the money. He directed our national team with simplicity and knowledge, earning the respect of Argentine rugby.

'We contacted him when he was in South Africa coaching Eastern Province, he accepted [our offer] and got to work at once, first as a contributor and later as coach.'

Argentina's last result of 1998 was a 43–30 loss to Wales in Cardiff and they would open the next season with a two-Test series defeat at home to the same opponents, the World Cup hosts they were scheduled to meet in the opening match of the tournament later in the year.

There was temporary respite for Imhoff in a party atmosphere as the UAR celebrated its centenary in April 1999 with a match against the Rest of the World that doubled as an overdue farewell to Hugo Porta, who was 47 and played for the opening 18 minutes.

In total contrast, the June series, make or break for Imhoff, was marred by violence in the second Test and won 2–0 by Graham Henry's Wales side.

In a Jekyll and Hyde performance, Argentina played brilliantly in the first half of the first Test to go 23–0 up after 35 minutes but lost their way and their characteristic grit in the second half and their 36–26 defeat was a shock to their previously jubilant fans.

Still under a cloud from that defeat, Argentina were always second best to Wales in the second Test and lost 23–16. Annoyed at how much the Welsh scrum dominated the Pumas, prop Mauricio Reggiardo sparked a free-for-all when he punched Wales wing Dafydd James.

Imhoff was sacked but he had drawn up a World Cup squad list of 22 players that would cause controversy.

Pipo Méndez, who had got on well with Wyllie coaching the under-21 side, came back on board but his demand that he be allowed to alter some names on Imhoff's World Cup list led to another crisis.

Yet another issue that could have disrupted Argentina's plans even more was a UAR suspension for captain Pedro Sporleder and hooker Mario Ledesma for indiscipline at the end of a domestic match playing for their club Curupaytí when they were ruled to have insulted the referee after telling him he had had a very poor match.

After several appeals, the pair were allowed to join the squad on a tournament warm-up tour of Scotland and Ireland but only to train with them although they could play at the World Cup.

Lock Sporleder lost the captaincy which reverted to Lisandro Arbizu. Sporleder played at four World Cups between 1991 and 2003 but never as captain despite leading the Pumas in 20 of his 78 Tests.

Hooker/prop Federico Méndez missed out on the tournament with a leg injury although he would go on to play at a third World Cup in Australia in 2003 before retiring with 73 caps.

It is unclear if there were political motivations but it appeared Pipo Méndez did not want Pichot as the first choice scrum-half. Méndez told him and Nicolás Fernández Miranda they would play one warm-up Test each.

Wyllie backed Pichot, who wrote in his autobiography that the New Zealander urged him to show his best in the Murrayfield match. The Pumas' 31–22 victory was their first away to Scotland, winners of that year's Five Nations Championship, and the first on British soil.

Pichot, who had enemies in the UAR given his outspoken manner and status as a professional, was still dropped for the match in Dublin, Argentina's first against Ireland since 1990, where Fernández Miranda was given his start.

Argentina were 32–3 down with 25 minutes remaining and the coaches made some changes, among them Pichot for Fernández Miranda, who did not hide his anger at being replaced. Pichot scored two tries as the Pumas fought back to within eight points, losing 32–24.

Back home, when Méndez dropped two backs who were on the World Cup list penned by Imhoff he was faced with a player revolt and the UAR with complaints from the provincial unions of the two excluded players.

Méndez, feeling a lack of support from the UAR given that they regarded him as number two to Wyllie, resigned two weeks before the team's departure for the World Cup and this left the New Zealander in sole charge at the tournament.

In an interview with *La Nación* days after resigning, Méndez gave three reasons for his decision: a lack of respect by the UAR for Pumas great Pochola Silva, leaving him out of the World Cup coaching staff, the humiliation of his own perceived demotion to assistant coach and what he called a contrived face-off between Buenos Aires and other provincial unions over the composition of the squad.

'All is good with Alex on a personal level. The arguments we had didn't have anything to do with this conflict,' he said.

New dawn

THE PUMAS MET hosts Wales in the opening match of the 1999 World Cup and lost 23–18 with all their points coming from the boot of fly-half Gonzalo Quesada, who went on to finish the tournament as top scorer with 102 points.

Their next rivals in Pool D were Samoa, bête noire of the two previous tournaments, but this time the Pumas came back from 16–3 down at half-time to win 32–16, setting a World Cup record that still stands for the best second-half recovery.

Lock Alejandro Allub scored a try and the rest of the points came from Quesada's eight penalties and one drop goal.

A 33–12 win over Japan, including Pichot's first World Cup try, qualified Argentina for a quarter-final play-off against Pool E runners-up Ireland by virtue of being the best third-placed team in the five pools.

The teams had to travel to the small, northern French town of Lens for what was a dramatic 28–24 upset victory for the Pumas, the first clash of a special World Cup rivalry.

A kicking duel between Ireland fly-half David Humphreys and Quesada stood at 24–18 to the Irish with seven minutes remaining on the clock.

The Pumas had been behind throughout the match, 15–9 at half-time and 21–9 by the fourth minute of the second half, but found new wind with a key change in the backs when Wyllie introduced Felipe Contepomi at fly-half and withdrew Quesada to full back.

'The idea was to give the team a new dynamic and get out of our system because we had become predictable,' said captain Arbizu. 'We needed to be more creative and take more initiative.'

A fast move down the line initiated by the fresh Contepomi went out to wing Diego Albanese who sped to the corner beating the Irish cover and diving to score with Quesada's conversion putting Argentina in front for the first time at 25–24.

Quesada kicked his seventh penalty one minute from time for a match tally of 23 to give the Pumas a four-point lead.

With Ireland needing more than a three-point score to win, the Pumas kept the Irish at bay for a tantalising, seemingly eternal nine minutes, three more than the additional time announced after 80, before the final whistle went.

The exhausted Pumas, called upon to play again at Lansdowne Road four days later, lost their quarter-final 47–26 to France but this did not dampen their joy at having overcome their jinx.

It was one of the great World Cup matches. 'Fast and loose and exhilarating quarter-final, featuring the Pumas as we've never seen them before and the French that we'd forgotten,' said the *Sunday Times*.

France raced into a 17–0 lead in the opening ten minutes before the Pumas got a grip and turned it into a classic of attacking rugby with dramatic twists even if the French were always ahead.

Pichot, always incisive from the base of the scrum, led the fightback with his second try of the tournament from five yards.

The French pulled away again when Arbizu's kick was charged down by Émile Ntamack and the wing scored but the Pumas centre then hit back with a try of his own leaving France with a 27–20 lead at half-time.

The Pumas pack were dominant for a good part of the second half and a penalty from Felipe Contepomi, on for Quesada, put the Pumas within four points at 30–26 down with 13 minutes remaining.

Then the exertions of three Tests in a week (Japan 16 October, Ireland 20 October and France 24 October) took their toll on the Pumas and France pulled away for a deserved victory although with a score that was not a true reflection of the difference between the sides that afternoon.

Early Loffreda years

MARCELO LOFFREDA TOOK charge of the team from 2000 and, in a quirk of the international calendar arranged months earlier, they played Ireland at home in their next Test match, winning 34–23.

But the overall journey to the tournament in Australia in 2003 was a roller coaster as a talented generation of Pumas began finding their feet in a new world with more professionals in the team but far from home, limiting the squad's time together.

In 2000, Argentina lost a series 2–0 in Australia, came very close to beating South Africa at home in a 37–33 defeat and lost 19–0 to England at Twickenham.

Progress in 2001 saw them claiming a first away win over Wales, 30–16, and also beating Scotland 25–16 on tour, then losing twice to New Zealand, 67–19 away before coming within a whisker of a first victory over the All Blacks but going down 24–20 at the River Plate stadium.

In June 2002, the Pumas beat France 28–27 in a one-off Test in Buenos Aires and 13 months later they got a first series win over the French, 10–6 and 33–32, at home before losing 26–25 to South Africa in Port Elizabeth.

At the World Cup, they again played the opening match and lost 24–8 to Australia in Sydney. Victories over Namibia and Romania sent them into a Pool A decider against Ireland in Adelaide which the Irish edged 16–15 to deny the Pumas a second consecutive quarter-final.

Argentina were upset with the match schedule which favoured Ireland despite the Pumas' victory over the Irish to reach the last eight in 1999.

Ireland, like all big-name teams, were scheduled to play only at weekends and had three more days' rest than the Pumas before their clash.

'We addressed this issue two years ago when we thought we were fifth after the World Cup but were dropped to eighth,' Loffreda said after the defeat. 'We wrote to the IRB asking why. They could not justify it to us, they just said it was "procedure" . . . It's the establishment.'

This time, it was Ireland who scored the only try, Alan Quinlan touching down midway through the first half following a break for the line by hooker Keith Wood and led 10–9 at half-time.

A drop goal by Ignacio Corleto put the Pumas ahead approaching the hour mark but Ronan O'Gara soon restored Ireland's lead and then extended it with two penalties and they saw out the win despite another Quesada penalty with six minutes remaining.

It was a huge disappointment for Argentina but also gave them the resolve to produce their best in 2007 – where they played in a third consecutive tournament opening match.

The first matches Argentina played after the 2003 World Cup were a series at home to Wales that finished 1–1 followed by a 41–7 loss to New Zealand in Hamilton in June 2004, matches that Pichot missed, playing for his new club Stade Français in the final stages of the French season.

A row with Loffreda could have split them for good with Pichot saying he had had enough of dignified defeats against the top teams. They made up and both strengthened their positions as captain and coach respectively.

The Pumas beat France 24–14 in Marseille that November and in 2005 they had another away win over Scotland. Then in 2006 they won a home series against Wales and were only narrowly beaten 25–19 by New Zealand in Buenos Aires.

Building on improved results, their tour of Europe at the end of that pre-World Cup year yielded a first win óver England at Twickenham, 25–18, a 23–16 victory over Italy and a 27–26 defeat by France in Paris.

SEVENTEEN

WYLLIE

———————— 🐾 ————————

ARGENTINA OWE THEIR World Cup breakthrough in 1999 to Alex 'Grizz' Wyllie, the former New Zealand back-row forward and coach, whom Agustín Pichot described two years later as 'the most important figure in the last five, six years in Argentine rugby.

'When he first came no one could understand him but he gave us rugby in depth and that's how we changed.'

Wyllie first worked for the Argentine union in 1992, spending two weeks in Buenos Aires helping coach Luis Gradín prepare the Pumas for a tour of Europe that ended with their first away win over France, a 24–20 upset victory in Nantes.

Wyllie had met Gradín the previous year when his All Blacks toured Argentina, winning a Test series 2–0.

Gradín became UAR president for the period 1996 to 2000, a particularly difficult time for Argentine rugby at the advent of open professionalism, and he asked Wyllie to lend a hand again. Wyllie accepted a three-year contract and worked with them throughout the 1999 World Cup cycle.

'I was technical advisor to the Pumas and José Luis Imhoff was their head coach but I also coached the under-21s. If it was a home series it was for a short time leading up to the series and while the games were being played and if the team was touring I was with them the whole time,' Wyllie says.

'They were very amateur with the things they did; it was obviously an amateur game out there. They were well behind a lot of other countries before they started to pay any of their top players.

'They had backs that could be very skilful, but they weren't always big; you could say it of all rugby now – backs have got much bigger because they've had to.

'They had a good strong scrum to be worked on. Their biggest problem was not being on time with so many things; they were pretty relaxed with a meeting – it wasn't important to be punctual . . . it was their make-up.'

On a tour of England in December 1996, Wyllie did not wait for a player who had overslept when it was time for the team bus to leave their hotel for the practice ground. It was a shock to the system but ultimately helped win Wyllie the respect of his players.

'It is probably more the make-up of the Argentine people in general to be pretty relaxed at times and they also have the Latin excitement, similar to the French, so it was probably more a matter of curtailing the excitement and constructively getting them to believe that they could perform as well as other teams and were as good as other top team players.'

Wyllie worked with some talented front-row forwards even after a new batch had come through to replace the best front row of the 1995 World Cup. Federico Méndez was still in the team but Pato Noriega had moved to Australia and Matías Corral to North America.

'We had a front row that could match anyone in the world: Roberto Grau, Mario Ledesma, Mauricio Reggiardo, Omar Hasan – who was a superb tenor too – and Federico Méndez, who could play anywhere in the front row. Also the young, at the time, Martín Scelzo.'

He did not get involved in the constant squabbling between the UAR and the Buenos Aires union URBA, who were staunchly amateur and angry with Gradín for allowing Méndez and Reggiardo to become the first professionals to play for the Pumas in 1996.

'[The amateur lobby] wanted control and once the game became professional the players could do what they liked and wanted to go overseas. Gus Pichot was one of those players who improved so much from being overseas.'

The build-up to the 1999 World Cup was severely disrupted by issues about who should be the head coach and the make-up of the squad.

This could so easily have led to yet another World Cup disappointment for Argentina, who had won only one of their nine matches in the first three tournaments.

Instead, Pipo Méndez, who had replaced the sacked Imhoff in July, resigned two weeks before the tournament leaving Wyllie in sole charge.

'I was in New Zealand when I heard over the radio, whilst driving around the lambing ewes, that the coach of Argentina had resigned,' said sheep farmer Wyllie.

'It came as a hell of a shock as I had no indication that there was anything wrong. Up until then I was never really consulted in final decisions so I was completely unaware of anything that may have been going on. So I became selector/coach.

'I didn't know what politics were going on behind the scenes as far as Imhoff was concerned and was happy to work with both José and Pipo.'

However, Méndez had shown a preference at scrum-half for Nicolás Fernández Miranda, who played for his club Hindú, over Pichot, whom Wyllie favoured. Both were given a Test each on a World Cup warm-up tour with Pichot picked against Scotland.

'We beat Scotland and then went to Ireland and that was when they put Nico in at half back.

'I believe that in Test matches you always have to field your best team, even if it means some players don't get a game. Nico was a very good half back, don't get me wrong, but Pichot had that X factor and was a great team man and it was just unfortunate they both had to be there at the same time.

'There are always times when two very good players are vying for the same position but the half-back position is a specialist one and I just felt Gus Pichot had the X factor.'

Wyllie had always held a back seat in the coaching system. 'I'd always thought of myself as number two and I'll give you an example.

'It was when we toured New Zealand in 1997 and got beaten 93–8. We'd been training there and I'd wanted to change the defensive pattern and they said no. I don't want to make a big thing of it but it's the sort of thing that had been happening all the way through.'

Imhoff had decided that instead of the wing picking up the attacking runs of the opposition's full back, the Pumas' marking would be wing on wing and full back on full back and Argentina fell to their worst ever defeat in the first Test with the All Blacks' full back Christian Cullen getting 20 metres of space to launch attacks.

'I said at the time, "If you carry on like this all you'll be doing is looking at the backside of Christian Cullen when he breaks through," and that's in fact what happened. They came back at half-time and said, "What can we do? How can we change our defence?" "It's a bit damn late now," I said. That was the sort of thing that they still had their own ideas about.

'They were coming to grips with professionalism and the way the game had changed. The Pumas' record was never bad; they were always a team to be reckoned with but then things changed quite a bit and I think they failed in some ways to go along with the changes.

'From the money side of it, there was nothing and the union was scraping along all the time. The kit for the national side, compared to other teams, wasn't great.

'But they didn't know any better. It was no different to when we were playing for nothing. You did it because you enjoyed it, loved the game and wanted to get on with it.'

Despite the 1997 debacle on tour in New Zealand, Wyllie had seen great promise in Argentina's game on his first tour with them to England the previous December when they lost the Test match at Twickenham 20–18 after a late Jason Leonard try.

The Pumas impressed the British media with a performance that had an England team full of big names like Will Carling, Jeremy Guscott, Martin Johnson and Lawrence Dallaglio in trouble.

The jumpers in the Argentina lineout – locks Pedro Sporleder and Germán Llanes and flanker Pablo Bouza – managed to often get the better of bigger and taller rivals but it was Johnson's catch in a late lineout inside Argentina's 22 and the pack's drive over the line that brought about Leonard's try.

Centre Eduardo Simone, who would go on to play for Bristol after the World Cup, regrets not realising he could have passed to Bouza for a certain try in the first half at the end of an attacking move involving 14 passes.

'We should have won that game,' says Wyllie. 'I don't like blaming referees but it was at a time when we completely controlled the scrum and we pushed over a couple of times and there should have been tries and in fact there should have ended up being a penalty try, either of them, that would have given us the win and they hung on.'

Play-off

SO, WITH WYLLIE in sole charge of the team at the 1999 tournament, the Pumas got their second, third and fourth World Cup wins, beating Samoa and Japan after an opening 23–18 loss to hosts Wales in their pool, then upsetting Ireland in the play-off for a quarter-final place.

Argentina's third meeting with the Samoans at a World Cup after defeats in 1991 and 1995 against the team then known as Western Samoa was crucial and they found themselves 16–3 down at half-time, 40 minutes from yet another disappointment.

'I was angry because they didn't play the way that I wanted them to play and we just had to get on top of them in the forwards and they didn't do that; they let the ball get loose.

'So I wasn't very happy with them at half-time. I probably said a few things and they might not have even understood what I said but they would have known I wasn't very happy.'

Lock Alejandro Allub scored a try in the second half and Samoan infringements allowed Gonzalo Quesada to take his kicking tally to 45 after two games in a 32–16 victory that is a World Cup record second-half comeback.

'The Samoans were getting a bit desperate and they made mistakes.'

Quesada would go on to finish as the tournament's top scorer with 102 points, most of them from 31 penalties in five matches.

'Even though it mightn't have been very attractive rugby, it was about keeping the ball in hand and wearing them down, keeping it reasonably tight,' Wyllie says.

'I don't really recall any of the players saying anything [at half-time]. Perhaps I didn't even give them a chance. They were doing things that were virtually the opposite of what we wanted to do.

'Maybe some were not used to learning to play differently against different teams. We had to redo our game completely and get back to the way we should have been doing it.'

Wyllie found himself doing a lot of man management when he was in sole charge of the team.

'In the first game against Wales, I'll never forget when we went out into the middle of the stadium before the game. I looked around and quite a few of them had tears rolling down their cheeks and I thought hell, what have we got here?

'They were overcome with everything so I had to get them

into the dressing room as quickly as possible. It was so much for them to take in, where they were and what they were going out to try and do.'

Against Japan, Argentina played 'fairly tight as well because the Japanese are a team that like to run, loosen the game up and run around a bit.

'Looking back at Argentina's record in World Cup games, they'd only won one and they'd had a lot of opportunities and I remember listening to when they were playing England (in 1995) and they had England on the ropes at one stage and England came back in the last quarter of an hour, twenty minutes and beat them.

'So it was a matter of trying to get their heads right about winning games. It's about saying it's all right wanting to do certain things but you've got to actually get more points than the opposition.

'You have to realise what you're about. Against Ireland it wasn't about steamrolling the forwards because they (Ireland) could do that just as much so that try that came near the end of the game was done through the backs. You have different tactics for different teams.

'[Ireland] probably were thinking that after the way we had played some of the other games they would dominate us up front and that would be [Argentina's] game gone and we proved that wrong.'

Wales, Samoa and Argentina all finished with seven points after two wins and one defeat each in a tight pool, with Japan getting none. Argentina had the weakest scoring record so went through to the quarter-final play-offs as the best third-placed team of the five pools.

'We had to play Ireland, who were coached by Warren Gatland, at Lens, beating them 28–24. One of the things I was questioned about was when I made the late change of Gonzalo Quesada to go from first five (fly-half) to full back and for Felipe Contepomi to come on as first five.

'I remember our manager José Rolandi asking me if I had got that right, to which I replied yes, in a hurry as time was running out. The opportunity arose for a well-practised move to be executed which won us the game coming from behind on the scoreboard.

'For the remaining eight or so minutes, which seemed like a bloody hour, our defence was outstanding to keep Ireland out.

'It was great to get as far as we did but it really was too much of an ask to expect the team to recover enough to play three hard games in a week with travel – to play in Dublin against France, who then went on to beat the All Blacks.' France then lost the final to Australia.

Socks

WYLLIE, A GUEST at Pichot's farewell as a player at his club CASI in 2009, took pride in Argentina's achievement under his guidance and fondly remembers his players.

'It's always good if you've got a bit of knowledge that you think you can pass on and if a team is willing to listen and take things on board and you see an improvement and you see things happening. It's good to be able to do something for rugby-playing nations.'

Commenting on Felipe Contepomi's assertion that he had learnt from Wyllie that it was important to wear your socks up to protect your calf muscles from injury, Wyllie said many players used shin pads during his time.

'They used to wear shin pads, that sort of thing, well I didn't but if somebody had their socks down and you were in a ruck you'd probably try to rake his leg to show him he should have his socks up but my father always used to say even if you can't play the game, look as though you can and look tidy.

'But there's no doubt that I said that. Gus [Pichot] was the one I kept on at about it because he always had his socks around his ankles. It was just a thing that I had, that I thought it looked untidy.

'All those players, I often wonder what happened to them: Albanese, he was a great little player with a big heart, the Contepomis had the ability to be great players, there was Simone and Corleto and Lobbe, and Allub, who finished because of his health, and Pedro Sporleder who was in finance. There was a hell of a lot of talent there.

'And then there was Pablo Camerlinckx, who wasn't always available because of his work commitments. I didn't know about him being dropped (from the 1999 World Cup squad). He was a hell of a good player, and he would have been a great player to have at the World Cup; there was quite a bit of politics involved, wasn't there.'

Wyllie was sorry to see Pichot lose in World Rugby's 2020 election for the position of chairman.

'I was disappointed that he didn't win because I think he could have changed a lot of things with his outlook on the game. I thought France and Italy with their Latin background could have supported him.

'He wasn't afraid to say things. Like now, he was quite positive. And in doing so he has gone against his mate in administration (Bill Beaumont).

'I do think he would be a breath of fresh air.

'If you look at what's happened to the game, the number of people – and I have spoken to one or two of them – who have been watching rugby going back a few years, they have said it is deteriorating with the way it is being played.

'That goes for crowds watching it – it's not as spectacular as it used to be. That's the sort of thing Pichot would like to see change, I am sure.

'His attitude; he was also very quick, read the game well.'

Wyllie's reaction to Argentina's first victory over New Zealand in the 2020 Rugby Championship encapsulates his opinion of the game today.

'It was much about what has happened in rugby all around, but it's now all about defence.'

Wyllie recalls the 1959 Lions who toured New Zealand when he was a teenager as one of the best sides he saw, better than the 1971 vintage he played against.

'The way they ran and made breaks, to me that's what the game is all about, running with the ball and scoring tries. Now it's stand up flat and knock each other over.'

The first Argentina team: the side that faced John Raphael's British tourists in the first Test match played by a representative Argentine team on 12 June 1910 in Buenos Aires. Their skipper, with the greying hair and hands clasped in the centre of the photo, is Oswald Gebbie, the former Edinburgh Academicals centre. Missing from the team photo is the former Springbok captain, Barry Heatlie.

A packed crowd at the Gimnasia y Esgrima Club Stadium in Buenos Aires
watch a tense moment during the third Test against the 1927 British Lions.

Action from the Test match staged at the Gimnasia
y Esgrima Club Stadium in Buenos Aires in 1936
when the touring British side wore the three-lions
crest on their blue jerseys.

Héctor 'Pochola' Silva (centre), who at 20 was hailed on the 1965 tour to South Africa as so good that had he been South African he would have been a Springbok for the quality of his all-round game. Silva is flanked by two fellow veterans of that groundbreaking tour, who went on to coach the Pumas, Luis Gradín (left) and Bernardo Aitor Otaño, the 1965 captain.

An iconic try in Pumas history: centre Marcelo Pascual dives over to score against the Junior Springboks in 1965, a game which the tourists famously won 11–6.

Martin Sansot makes a break during the Pumas' 24–13 victory over Australia in Buenos Aires in 1979. *Rex Gowar*

Ernesto Ure crosses to score during Argentina's first win over France in 1985 as the great Serge Blanco and Philippe Sella watch on helplessly. *Enrique Shore*

Captain Hugo Porta breaks away from Peter FitzSimons and Brad Burke during Argentina's 1986 tour game against New South wales at the Concorde Oval in Sydney. Centres Fabián Turnes and Diego Cuesta Silva are poised for Porta's next move. *Brendan Read/ Getty Images*

Right: Hugo Porta attacks with a punt during Argentina's first win over France in June 1985. *Rex Gowar*

Below: Prop Diego Cash dives to tackle Dave Loveridge as the All Blacks scrum-half passes to Wayne Smith during Argentina's 21–21 draw with New Zealand in November 1985. *Rex Gowar*

Flankers Pablo Garretón (left) and Jorge Allen – who both captained Argentina –in action against France in Buenos Aires in June 1988. *Rex Gowar*

Santiago Meson, Marcelo Loffreda and Guillermo De Castillo in action in 1994.

Alex Wyllie oversees a training session before Argentina's opening 1999 World Cup match in Cardiff. *David Rogers/Allsport*

The players celebrate the final whistle of the 1999 Rugby World Cup quarter final play-off against Ireland at the Stade Felix Bollaert, Lens, France, winning 28–24. *Alex Livesey/Allsport*

Agustín Pichot makes a break against England at Twickenham in November 2000. *Dave Rogers /Allsport*

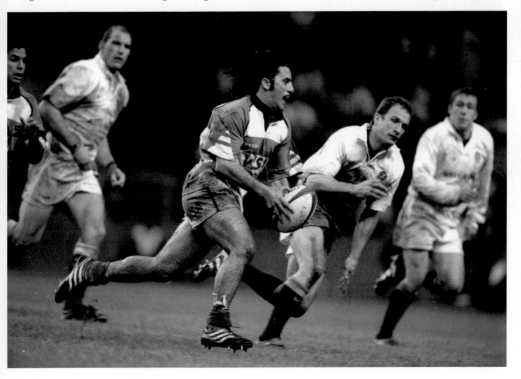

Frederico Todeschini slides in to score during Argentina's victory over England at Twickenham in November 2006. *Action Images/Andrew Couldridge*

An outstanding Argentine performance shocked 2007 World Cup tournament hosts France in their opening pool match in Paris. *Alamy*

Juan Martin Hernandez ('El Mago') was in imperious form at the 2007 World Cup. *Daniel Bardou/Alamy*

Felipe Contepomi breaks through the tackle of France's David Marty during a virtuoso performance that helped guide Argentina to victory in the third/fourth play-off at the 2007 World Cup. *Action Images/Jason O'Brien*

Juan Figallo (3) and Agustín Creevy savour Argentina's victory in Auckland in 2011 that put Scotland to the sword for a second consecutive World Cup as the Pumas progressed to the quarter-finals to face hosts New Zealand. *Anthony Phelps/ Alamy*

After years of campaigning to join the SANZAR nations in an annual competition, Argentina were finally rewarded when the inaugural Rugby Championship kicked off in 2012. Here Gonzalo Camacho tries to escape the clutches of Marcell Coetzee at Newlands Stadium in Cape Town. *Alamy*

Scrum-half Martín Landajo celebrates as Argentina enjoy a landmark victory over South Africa in Durban in August 2015, winning 37–25. *Alamy*

Juan Imhoff flies in to score during Argentina's demolition of Ireland in the 2015 World Cup quarter-final at the Millennium Stadium. *Alamy*

The greatest victory in the Pumas' history? After a build-up that saw the Argentine players train in isolation at home and then in their team hotel because of Covid-19 restrictions, Pablo Matera led the way in his side's stunning victory over New Zealand in the 2020 Rugby Championship game in Parramatta, Australia. *Alamy*

Marcos Kremer makes a break during the Pumas' victory over
Wales at the Principality Stadium in July 2021. *Reuters/Rebecca Naden*

EIGHTEEN

LOFFREDA

'I never thought of quitting; that's part of what rugby taught me – to persevere and be constant in my efforts.'
Marcelo Loffreda

THE PUMAS CAREER of Marcelo 'Tano' Loffreda, a rugged outside centre in his playing days and an astute, persevering coach afterwards, spans more than four decades from his 1978 debut.

It was a period that marked Argentina's turbulent journey from a strong team of amateurs capable on their day of living with the best to cementing a place among the elite despite a slump in the 1990s brought on by their struggles to get to grips with the transition to a professional game.

Loffreda could have taken part in five of the first six World Cups but was denied any chance as a player at the first three before his ultimate achievement – drawing partly from the experience of those disappointments – in coaching the Pumas to their best position as winners of the bronze medal in France in 2007.

He made his Pumas debut in Argentina's 13–13 draw with England at Twickenham in October 1978 and went on to play regularly for five years in the side led by Hugo Porta, sharing a fine centre partnership with San Isidro Club (SIC) teammate Rafael Madero.

He was part of a 24–13 first Test victory at home to Australia in 1979, another 19–19 draw with England in Buenos Aires in 1981 and a first ever away victory, 18–3 over the Wallabies, in 1983.

He also played for the South American Jaguars who upset South Africa 21–12 in Bloemfontein in the second Test of their 1982 tour, the day after Argentine forces invaded the disputed Malvinas/Falkland Islands sparking the war with Britain in the South Atlantic and the cessation of diplomatic relations.

This did not stop the Pumas touring France at the end of 1982 and Australia in mid-1983.

Loffreda's work commitments prevented him from touring South Africa again with the Jaguars in 1984, opening the door to a talented young centre partnership in Diego Cuesta Silva, who also played for SIC, and Porta's Banco Nación club mate Fabián Turnes.

This new pairing took centre stage in Argentina's brilliant 1985 season that included the first win over France (24–16) and the draw with New Zealand (21–21).

Loffreda, who also missed a tour of Australia in 1986, was overlooked for the 1987 World Cup squad, his first disappointment though not the biggest, which was to come in 1991.

'It was hurtful to be left out, having been a first choice for the Pumas for a long time and played a lot of matches. I had a lot of difficulty getting over it and getting on with my life. We were all amateurs but we put a lot of time into rugby besides having a separate professional activity,' Loffreda said, though he was philosophical about it.

'But I also learnt from it. It was an experience that helped when I was coach, above all when I had to make decisions over players who weren't going to get on my final team list, how to tell them that they hadn't been selected.'

Loffreda said coaches at that time tended to opt for youth, enthusiasm and the physical fitness of players.

'Fabián Turnes was a very talented player with impressive skills and Diego Cuesta Silva, who is my friend from playing many years together at SIC, was a powerful player, very fast, much faster than me and younger if we compare the two [centre] partnerships.'

Loffreda did not object to their selection by coaches Héctor Silva and the experienced Angel Guastella, who liked to play fast, getting the ball out to the wings. But he feels they also picked too many players with hardly any international experience.

He was back at the end of the year, playing outside Turnes with Cuesta Silva on the wing and Madero at full back in the series victory at home to Australia (19–19 and 27–19) after which Porta retired for the first time.

Another reshuffle without Porta had Madero at fly-half when the Pumas beat France 18–6 in the second Test to share the 1988 series.

Loffreda was captain when Argentina shared a home series with England in August 1990, winning the second Test 15–13.

But then there was a change of coach with Luis Gradín taking charge and Loffreda was dropped less than three months later for the tour of the British Isles when Porta returned to lead a new young side that lost heavily to England and Scotland.

'That did hurt a lot. I had been captain the year before and I was 30 going on 31, an ideal age to play and give the team a lot of experience. It was a shock, their wanting an abrupt change, and then it all ends up going wrong, but that's an Argentine issue, not just in rugby, wiping the slate clean, lacking confidence in a more sensible vision; it's our country's history. We get it wrong again and carry the same stone all the time.

'This was good for when it was my turn to coach the team so I didn't make the same mistake. For me it was very important to count on mature players who might have had some enriching experience to share with the team, whether they were first choice or reserves.

'Regardless of such decisions affecting me, I saw them as big mistakes and having experienced them myself, they marked me even more.

'Coaches in general were too quick to bet on good talents, kids with a lot of potential, many with more promise than anything else. Some really starred as in the case of Turnes and Cuesta Silva, who were exceptional, two first-rate internationals. And there were players who had given the team a lot and could still do so but were discarded.'

The three World Cups that Loffreda missed out on were the three that Cuesta Silva, who won 63 caps between 1983 and 1995, played. The pair played together for Argentina 17 times, seven in the 1990s when Turnes was playing in Italy.

Two decades later, Argentina's winning start to the 2007 World Cup owed a lot to an almost ideal convergence of the experience of the leaders and the talent of younger players. 'It was a very favourable mix.'

Loffreda didn't play for the Pumas again until 1994 when he was immediately restored to the captaincy. He led a winning home series against Scotland (16–15 and 19–17) and closed out his international career on tour in South Africa taking his caps total to 46.

Another change of leadership at the UAR, whose four-yearly elections fell the year before World Cups, brought in new coaches for 1995 and Loffreda's last chance of a World Cup at 35 was gone.

Loffreda bowed out as a player after helping Buenos Aires upset France 29–26 during the French tour of Argentina in 1996 and became coach of SIC and later Buenos Aires.

Head Coach

WITH HIM AS coach, SIC won the first division title in 1997 and 1999, the year his Buenos Aires side upset Wales 31–29 after an amusing episode with New Zealander Graham Henry, then Wales's coach, that was the start of a friendship between the two.

'I went to watch Wales train, so as to spy on them a bit. I stand at the side of the pitch and Graham Henry is in the middle and I see him go over to their manager who then approaches me and says, "How are you?" So I reply, "Hello, I came to see you practise because it interests me – I'm a rugby fanatic."

'"Yes, we know you're a rugby fanatic and that you train Buenos Aires and on Saturday we're playing against you," he says. I didn't know where to hide . . . "If you want to carry on watching there's no problem."'

Within months, Loffreda was training SIC, Buenos Aires and Argentina simultaneously 'and I also had my job as a civil engineer so it got quite complicated and I ended up putting all my energy into the Pumas.'

The eight-year journey from taking charge of the Pumas in 2000 to reaching the 2007 World Cup semi-finals was a roller coaster for Loffreda and his sidekick Daniel Baetti, who had won 15 caps as a full back and scrum-half.

'It was very difficult to build a proper team. We felt a lot of impotence because we couldn't count on the players most of the time.

'And we couldn't focus on lasting tactical or strategic issues because we usually had to change players [depending on their availability].

'So we had to see who we were getting to apply short-term tactics for a specific Test match. There was little continuity; we basically depended on the clubs to release the players for us.

'If I have to summarise that period, on the one hand we felt we had a lot of capacity but on the other we ended up quite limited to what we could get during each Test window we faced.'

A calendar decision made months before Argentina's 1999 World Cup win over Ireland and Loffreda's appointment happened to determine that Argentina would face the Irish again as the first opponents of the Loffreda and Baetti era. The Pumas won 34–23 in Buenos Aires in June 2000.

But that did not immediately bring in a succession of positive results although the Pumas ran South Africa close in a 37–33 defeat at the River Plate stadium that November.

The next season started with a sweep of the Pan American Championship, beating Uruguay, the United States and Canada in North America. Then a crushing 67–19 loss to New Zealand in Christchurch in June and a 24–20 home defeat by the All Blacks in December bookended wins over Wales (30–16) and Scotland (25–16) on a tour of Britain.

A 28–27 win against France in June 2002 was Loffreda's first of six in seven meetings as coach against the French and was followed by a series victory, also at home, over the same opponents a year later. A week later Argentina came within a whisker of beating South Africa for the first time in a 26–25 defeat in Port Elizabeth.

Argentina's fate at the 2003 World Cup in Australia was decided by one point in a 16–15 defeat by Ireland.

Having failed to reach the quarter-finals in Australia, Loffreda and Baetti were set to call it a day, thinking it was the end of a cycle of limited achievement but in which they had given their all.

'Of course, if I'd been told, "You've had four years, the team failed to qualify for the quarter-finals, that's it," I would have gone home quite calm and content.

'But it wasn't like that and we agreed with Daniel Baetti that this team had enormous potential, very good players, a fine head with an amateur grounding and playing as professionals which was a near-perfect formula. That gave us a lot of motivation to press on.'

The UAR headed now by Gradín, and with Gringo Perasso on the selection board, had seen good signs from Loffreda's tenure and offered the coaches a contract extension.

'It came as a surprise and we had to think about it at family level because it had all been *ad honorem* and I had my profession as an engineer so I had to discuss it at work to see if they would back me when I had to go on tour.

'It was quite a hard decision but I was able to accept and we then tried to change some things we had done up to 2003 although there were others we couldn't change because the players had their contracts with their clubs and that famous Rule 9 was in place.'

The International Rugby Board (now World Rugby) had created the rule obliging clubs to release their international players only for the Test windows in June and November and international tournaments like the Six Nations, Tri-Nations and World Cups.

'It would continue to be difficult to build the team but we had got the hang of it so what we did was hold training get-togethers in Europe because the majority were in Europe and that was going to be cheaper and would mean not taking them from the clubs for a full week. They would get them back within three days.'

Loffreda and Baetti were not paid, only the team doctor, physios and fitness coaches. Their successor in 2008, Santiago 'Tati' Phelan, who was coach through the 2011 World Cup cycle and into the Rugby Championship which Argentina joined in 2012, was the UAR's first paid coach.

'We were the last rung on the ladder of the amateur era when the players weren't paid either.'

The Pumas squad that went to the 1999 World Cup had five professionals including Pichot who had moved from Richmond to Bristol, and captain Lisandro Arbizu, who was with Brive.

Over the next four years the exodus of Argentines to the top leagues in Europe, mainly France, grew fast and the exiles in the 30-man squad in Australia in 2003 numbered 16. By the 2007 World Cup, the 31-man squad had only seven home-based amateurs.

Failure to progress to the knockout phase of the 2003 World Cup hit hard and could have split the leading players and coaches.

There were recriminations, one being how Loffreda had handled what was a grossly unfavourable match schedule in Pool A which Argentina shared with hosts Australia as the top seeds, Ireland, Romania and Namibia.

Despite having finished better placed than Ireland in 1999, Argentina had three days less rest for their pool decider in Adelaide which the Irish won 16–15.

After two matches each, the Pumas had lost to Australia in the tournament's opener in Sydney before thrashing Namibia while the Irish had won first against Romania, then Namibia on 19 October. Argentina beat the Romanians on 22 October and met Ireland in their crunch match on 26 October.

Loffreda felt they should have been consulted when the match dates for their pool were arranged.

'Australia and Ireland were the teams that got the greater ease despite the fact that in 1999 we had reached the quarter-finals. For some reason [the organisers] favoured Ireland in the drawing up of the fixtures, not so much in the match order as the rest time between matches. In hindsight that worked against us though at the time you just face what's next.

'As a player and a coach I experienced situations where it was clear there was a difference in the treatment of one team and the other. You feel a bit disadvantaged. The weaker team can take it as an adversity and take strength from it, but I still think the match ends up not being on a level playing field. You can take it as a motivation but in the end it's still unfair.

'I really don't know if it was premeditated but they are things that happen to one team and not the other and end up being a little suspicious.'

Also, players were unhappy with the coaches' decision to field a majority of reserves against their two weaker opponents which might have kept the best players fresh for the key clash with Ireland but denied them match practice in tournament conditions.

'There were two very distinct groups [in the squad]: the old guard that I didn't want to discard because I felt we needed their experience, such as Fede Méndez, Pedro Sporleder, Arbizu, and then there were the younger ones who also had a certain experience like Agustín, Felipe, Manuel (Contepomi), Corleto, who maybe clashed a bit with the older ones.'

The 2003 squad did not have the harmony of 2007. 'It's an extra burden [that as coach] you have to try to reduce, minimise and even avoid it affecting the tension and concentration of the players.

'The mental aspect is crucial when you have to play a Test or a World Cup match. Any distraction or loss of energy that takes your focus off the game ends up being a disadvantage that shows in a player's performance. It affects decision-making. They are subtle differences that end up deciding a match.'

Lions

LOFFREDA'S SECOND FOUR-year cycle began with a 50–44 win over Wales in Tucumán. The series was drawn when the Welsh won the second Test 35–20 in Buenos Aires. Later in the year the Pumas notched a fourth consecutive victory over France, 24–14 in Marseille.

In May 2005, Argentina had an unusual but very welcome fixture, invited to give Clive Woodward's British and Irish Lions a warm-up in Cardiff prior to their series in New Zealand.

As the match was not on an official international date, few European clubs were prepared to release their Argentine players, particularly the French who were at a critical stage of their championship, and Loffreda was not entitled to appeal citing Rule 9.

So the team that faced the Lions was very much a Pumas B side although captained by Felipe Contepomi, who was released by Leinster.

Denied at least 15 leading Pumas, Loffreda managed to entice front-row forwards Federico Méndez and Mauricio Reggiardo out of international retirement to help him build a competitive side.

Lisandro Arbizu, who had recovered from the injury that put him out of the 2003 World Cup, also played at the tail end of his Pumas career.

Loffreda purposely emphasised all these supposed weaknesses at a press conference before the coaches and home-based section of the squad left Buenos Aires for Cardiff.

'We showed as weak a face as possible so the Lions and Clive Woodward as their coach would think it was going to be an easy match, kind of a practice, and we had other intentions which were to go and play as equals and try to win.'

The Pumas very nearly did win, a penalty in added time by the infallible Jonny Wilkinson – in his first outing since England's 2003 World Cup final win in Australia – salvaging a 25–25 draw for the Lions, who had been behind throughout the match at the Millennium Stadium.

The match featured several players who would be on the fringe of the 2007 team, not least fly-half Federico 'Ninja' Todeschini, who kicked 20 points, the same as his opposite number Wilkinson.

Argentina's desperation for a place in an annual international tournament led Loffreda to voice a desire he and his players had been talking about for some time: to seek admission to the Six Nations, given that many of their best players played their club rugby in Europe.

He made his first pitch in an exclusive interview with me for Reuters on the evening before the Pumas played the Lions and it became the main topic in Loffreda's post-match press conference the following evening.

'I recall telling you then that, without having yet made a deal or agreed with the UAR politicians, we were available to come and play the Six Nations, always as a visiting team, ceding home advantage. We were very keen to compete at international level and knew we were capable.'

The year, which had begun with a 68–36 win over Japan, had mixed results with a 30–29 home defeat by Italy for a shared series after winning the first Test 34–21, then losses to South Africa and Samoa at home but wins against Scotland and Italy on tour.

The 2006 season was much better, starting with a home series win over Wales (27–25 and 45–27) in the June Test window and a first away victory over England, 25–18 at Twickenham in November when they also beat Italy 23–16 in Rome and lost 27–26 to France at Saint-Denis.

It was a different story off the pitch, the Pumas coming up against the destabilising force of a hostile new administration at the UAR with president Alejandro Risler and secretary Raúl 'Ruso' Sanz, who had won the elections before the northern hemisphere Test window in 2005.

'Towards the end of 2005 the board changed and a new group took charge with Risler and Sanz, two guys with strong personalities and firm ideas about staying totally amateur.

'I had a good relationship with the UAR until 2005 because on the board there were people who had a good opinion of me and knew me quite well, one of them being Gringo Perasso, who had been my coach as a player at SIC.

'It was a huge culture clash because during Perasso's tenure, relations were much friendlier, aware that the transition had to be made [to professionalism]. Risler and Sanz put sticks in the wheel; they made things very difficult.

'On the one hand, the squad preparing for 2007 felt a lot of tension but on the other it united them even more and the staff too.

'Sanz had a lot of experience as a trainer [at club level]. He's a very, very troublesome character, very controversial who got into the core of the national team without holding a specific position and he managed almost everything there. He didn't get involved in the technical side but in organisational aspects and arrangements with the players regarding economic matters he was always making things difficult.

'To be completely fair, the truth is the UAR had scant resources to cover the players' needs because they demanded some bonuses and expenses they had got with the previous board to help the amateur players.

'But there was [previously] a clear attitude of solidarity from the UAR, who had created what was known as the Fondo Puma (Puma Fund) with what was earned through advertising and commercial contracts divided up equally in relation to the number of games played, a good arrangement made with the players.'

This became an issue with Risler and Sanz, a constant battle because they questioned how much the various specialists attached to Loffreda and Baetti, who worked *ad honorem*, should be paid for their services, such as the team doctor, the physiotherapist, the fitness coach.

'I was the staff's representative, so I had to argue for their pay because if not they might quit. The same happened to the players with the Puma Fund. At that time there were players in Argentina getting expenses to be able to keep training over and above what they were doing with their clubs.

'We had to keep the 50 per cent of amateurs at a level with the pros so they were ready for whatever the team might want of them. They were still playing in Argentina but needed professional preparation so we had arranged for them to do extra work twice a week and needed to pay the fitness personnel.

'At the end of 2005 we had a meeting with them (Risler and Sanz) and others on the board and they started setting out how they wanted to go forward and I realised it wasn't going to be at all easy to reach agreement with them because they were totally against professionalism, though in time they softened, realising the benefits.

'It was really hard for me and Daniel, and Agustín also had to fight a lot – he was the face of the players. All this on top of actually working on the team, training, arranging meetings, keeping the players in contact – it [2006] was a tough year.'

The players decided to stage a protest against Risler's administration and the victory over England turned into the ideal setting.

At the post-match dinner at Twickenham attended by both teams and 300 guests, Pichot spoke of what the victory meant for Argentina but when Risler stood up to speak, the players all rose quietly from their seats and left the hall, a plan Loffreda had asked them to keep low key.

'The players had wanted to whistle Risler and I told them, "Guys, please don't go and whistle at him. If you want to do something that won't provoke a rupture you get up respectfully, silently and you leave, but no whistling or anything like that."'

In Rome, the following week, there was another serious incident that led to another team protest.

When the squad returned from a training session they were met with the news that former Pumas and Wallabies prop Pato Noriega was on his way from Buenos Aires to join the staff.

'I couldn't believe it,' said Loffreda laughing.

'"Anyone know about this?" I asked.

'It was a complete surprise and it was a decision made by Sanz with Noriega unaware that none of the coaching staff or squad knew, or that's what he said.'

Noriega was a part of the Argentina set-up because Loffreda had appointed him as coach of Argentina A. 'But that was not the Pumas.

'I confronted him at the hotel and said, "Tell me what you're doing here," and that's when he said that Sanz had informed him to come because he wanted to look at a matter of video analysis. It was all a bit confusing but when the players heard about it they also took a firm stand.

'If certain conditions we had been demanding were not implemented, the team would not turn out against Italy.'

They did. Argentina beat the Italians 23–16 and a week later lost to France 27–26 in Paris, the only defeat in seven meetings with the French in the eight years Loffreda was their coach.

A meeting was held on the eve of the match in Rome to iron things out and Sanz, no doubt realising Argentina needed calm with the World Cup fast approaching and that he couldn't bend the Pumas staff and team, suddenly said the UAR would give them all they needed to prepare properly.

Funds were made available for the fitness preparation of a squad of 41 including fringe players at the Athletes' Performance facility on the Andrews Institute campus in Pensacola, Florida.

'[Risler and Sanz] understood the World Cup was very close, that if they opposed us they weren't going to achieve anything, things would go badly, the players would resign and we, who knew the team so well, wouldn't be training them. There was more common sense, above all in Sanz.'

This led to Sanz arranging practice games against Leicester and Northampton in England in February and the French Barbarians in Biarritz in March.

The World Cup season began with a home series victory over Ireland (22–20 and 16–0) and a win against Italy (24–6) in the June Test window before embarking for France via a warm-up in Cardiff.

Wales beat Argentina 27–20 in that Test at the Millennium Stadium in August and some doubts crept in among observers as to Argentina's form for the tournament.

More serious was what happened to centre Martín Gaitán, who fainted in the changing room after the Test and turned out to have a problem with an artery and underwent surgery at the University Hospital in Cardiff.

Gaitán was discharged three days later but had to be replaced in the squad and never played again. He has been on the Pumas' coaching staff since.

'What happened to Gaitán was terrible. I'm not saying his life was at risk but it was a serious situation with all our attention focused on that and Agustín stayed overnight at the hospital keeping him company. He knew him well because they were from the same club, CASI.'

Several players arrived in Paris carrying minor injuries, including Gonzalo Longo who was injured in the final warm-up against a Belgian Invitation XV and missed the opening match of the World Cup, and Ignacio Corleto who only passed a late fitness test and went on to score the all-important try in the upset win over France.

'What we had tried to do from 2004 onwards was work on the players' mental fortitude and a lot of that was showing them how they had been overcoming adversity. We used that word a lot, adversity.'

Referees

LOFFREDA MADE SURE Argentina would compete on a level playing field by arranging a meeting with New Zealander Paddy O'Brien, then head of the IRB's Referee Board and Rugby World Cup Chief of Officials, before the tournament.

'It was very important for me to be able to speak to the referee before matches because that put us on an equal footing with our opponents. When we played against teams with a high ranking, to speak to the referee as equals in English was important to us. That way if there was any preference, even unconscious, the referee would come round to regarding both teams in the same way. I put it as a condition that we should be able to speak with the referee.'

Three days before Argentina faced France in the inaugural match, Loffreda paid O'Brien a visit at his Paris hotel.

'On 4 September, a few days before the opening match, I spoke to Paddy O'Brien, to go over some things we were sometimes penalised for in the lineout, the scrum, mauls too. There were issues that got repeated more than others, like feeding the ball into the scrum.

'We showed him some videos. I had a very good relationship with him. He was very good and gave us the space to do this, just us two coaches, calmly, without wanting to invade him.'

Englishman Tony Spreadbury took charge of the opening match.

Just as Argentina felt hard done by in decisions about World Cup match schedules, they also thought referees looked at them more closely than other teams, and so missed their opponents' smaller infringements. 'Those things have happened to us, though I won't give you the names of referees,' said Loffreda.

In fact, Loffreda had good reason to seek a meeting with O'Brien having found reasons to criticise the refereeing of the warm-up match in Cardiff three weeks earlier. 'I am worried about what will happen in the World Cup,' he said at the post-match news conference. 'If there is one rule for one team and another for the other team in the same game, we will have problems; we will have a lot of trouble.'

Loffreda, who said he had no complaint about the result, claimed the Pumas should have been awarded a penalty try late on when they laid siege to the Wales line, and accused the referee – Englishman Chris White – of coaching the Welsh team. 'I don't understand what happens with the interpretation of the rules because in some parts of the game there was one rule for Wales and another for Argentina.

'When we played against Ireland in Santa Fe two months ago the referee awarded a penalty try to Ireland when we collapsed the maul once, only once. Today there were clearly three times when Wales collapsed the maul. That's a penalty try.

'He was not refereeing a team, he was coaching a team. He said, maybe 45 or 50 times, "Reds, hands away."'

Loffreda recalled an occasion when the team bus taking the Pumas from their hotel to a match took 45 minutes on a route that they knew took half that time.

'Whether that was premeditated, I really don't know, but those are things that happen to one and not the other and end up being a little suspicious.'

Having beaten France and Ireland to win their pool and Scotland in their quarter-final, Argentina were brought down to earth by South Africa in their semi-final, an early interception try by Fourie du Preez sending the Springboks on their way to a 37–13 victory. 'Agustín was very upset about the defeat against South Africa but that doesn't mean he wasn't up for playing for third place.

'We told the players to go away: "We don't want to see you near the hotel or anywhere related to rugby; go with your families, wherever you want, make the most of these days and we'll get together again on Tuesday night."

'What we had to work on a lot was the mental aspect; some were very hurt emotionally by the defeat. That refreshed them.

'Could we have got to the final? Of course. We were very confident we could reach the final. We didn't say so publicly, I don't think anyone did . . . because to say so you have to be very careful, humble, measured, prudent and that's what reigned in the team and was one of their great merits, to seek strength inwardly.

'The almost superhuman effort the players made to have their heads in two such different places at the same time like an Argentine national team where everything is adversity, because we didn't have money, because we weren't part of any championship at world level, and then to go to a calm place which is your club where you have the right installations, professionalism, support and facilities. In that respect the world of rugby has shown a lot of recognition towards the Pumas.

'We experienced some very complex situations, especially with the [union] directors in the two and a half years leading up to the 2007 World Cup, having to juggle between authorities who didn't really know what they wanted and did everything they could for things to go badly for us and enjoying so much unity and good human and technical relations with the players.

'I never thought of quitting; that's part of what rugby taught me – to persevere and be constant in my efforts.'

NINETEEN

PICHOT

'Money is an instrument to become better, but
never an end. The day you play to earn money,
you've already lost your passion.'
Agustín Pichot

AGUSTÍN PICHOT BEGAN his fight against the odds very
early.

He was barely five months old and his mother Cristina was in
despair because her third child was pale, slept most of the time
and would only drink soy milk. Doctors couldn't work it out but
the family's maid said she had lost a nephew to such a condition
which she called goat's foot and said Cristina should see a healer.

Pichot's grandfather drives his daughter and the baby boy deep
into Buenos Aires province to meet a witch doctor. It's the middle
of winter and Cristina baulks when asked to undress the child but
does so and the healer, a Brazilian with long, dark braids wearing
a full-length white dress, makes a blue mark on his bottom and
gives his mother a mallow plant. 'Bring him to me every day for a
week and put mallow water in his bottle,' she says.

Grandfather and mother drive daily the 40 kilometres out to the healer's, who repeats the ritual each time: undressing the child, marking his back and bottom, praying and prescribing mallow.

A week later, little Agustín is the rosiest baby in the world and doesn't stop moving about and laughing, full of energy.

'My relationship with rugby starts with my dad and comes from my grandad who played for Obras Sanitarias and afterwards was a referee for a long time.

'It's as if I had no choice, but without choosing I already wanted that: to play for the Pumas. It's as if I was carrying the love, the passion my father had for rugby.'

Pichot is the middle boy in a family of four children, all involved, including his sister, in rugby and led by his late father Enrique, whom Agustín adored as his guiding light and whom the family lost to cancer aged 53 in 1999.

He made his first-team debut for Club Atlético San Isidro (CASI) in 1994 aged 19, helping them win promotion back to the URBA first division. The following year he helped CASI win the National Club Championship and URBA Sevens.

Pichot made his Pumas debut at 20 in Australia in April 1995, scoring a try in a 53–7 defeat by the Wallabies. Coach Alejandro Petra dropped him for the second Test.

He then became an unused squad member at the 1995 World Cup in South Africa, passing virtually unnoticed by anyone other than the Argentine journalists following the team and fans back home who had seen the talented scrum-half playing for CASI.

Argentine reporters covering the team's matches on the east coast of South Africa wondered when Petra might give Pichot his World Cup debut but the coach persisted with the steady, orthodox Rodrigo Crexell.

Petra's assistant Ricardo Paganini some years later admitted to Pichot that the pair had agreed to favour Crexell, who like Paganini was from Rosario, over Pichot, whose aggressive, unorthodox style, hovering around the base of the scrum or ruck looking to make a break rather than always playing the ball out immediately, was not to their liking.

This was a year and a half before he signed for Richmond, then in the English first division, at the dawn of professional rugby, and after winning the first seven of his 71 caps. He was then 21.

Former Leicester and England fly-half Les Cusworth (who some years later would become technical advisor to the Pumas) helped Pichot with his move.

'I was at a meeting in London in 1996 that John Kingston, director of rugby at Richmond and a good friend of mine, had with Pichot and Rolando 'Yanqui' Martin, who both joined the club,' says Cusworth.

'One thing you've got to admire about Agustín is he's not short of confidence, even in the early days. He's got a very shrewd head on his shoulders and he already knew what he was doing.

'I remember his mother was very grateful to me for making sure everything he did was to his benefit.'

Very early in Pichot's Richmond days, the week after a brilliant performance for the reserves against Leicester in which he orchestrated an unexpected victory, Tigers chairman Peter Wheeler came to Richmond asking to speak to him.

Pichot tells it like this in his book *Agustín Pichot, El Juego Manda* (the game rules), which is about his growth as a leader: 'He had a contract in his hand. "I don't understand," I tell him. "Well, we want you to come to play at Leicester, you'll get a big salary raise and what you earn there you won't spend because we give you a house and pay for your university which we know is important to you."

'"And what else?" I answer. The guy gets nervous and carries on: "Well, we've already spoken to your president and Richmond's coach and we've already agreed with them."

'"Ah, yes? What did you agree? Are they letting me go? Don't they want me here any more?" "No, well, we're paying the club big money." At that point I was really upset and losing it. I wanted to start crying with anger. What hurt me most was to hear that they were letting me go.

'Wheeler didn't know what was going on and carried on talking: "Agustín, do you want more money?" "Whom did you speak to?" I ask. "With your coach and Peter Moore."

'Peter Moore and I had a very good relationship, in fact I am still in touch with him today.

'"With me there is no such thing as 'I give you more money', Mr Wheeler." I thanked him and went straight off to look for Moore, who happened to be outside waiting.

'By then no one understood what was going on, because they didn't know me: Argentine, proud, arrogant, hot-tempered. I close the door of his office and ask, "What was that?" The English aren't used to outbursts.

'"No, the thing is that as you weren't happy and this is a great economic opportunity for the club, we thought you'd like . . ." "And you think it's okay to make a deal behind my back. I'm not a piece of meat!"

'The years go by and Moore is still laughing about that phrase and he always says the same to me: "You weren't there for the money, I wish we had more like you."

'I bang the table and don't stop: I won't leave here until I'm the best. I'll get taken out of Richmond feet first and it'll be when I want, not when you want. I have a contract and this is a rugby club.

'I closed the door and faced the coach: "I'm not leaving at all," and he holds his head in his hands. "Whoever pays me and whoever comes here, I'm staying until I'm the number one here."

'I was very visceral in those days. The coach looks at me and can't believe it. The look on his face seemed to say: "This kid's insufferable. What problem have I just bought myself? He's going to break my nut until he's number one." I go home crying, very annoyed and hurt.'

The chance to play came when Andy Moore hurt a finger at the beginning of 1998 and Pichot got a run of games in the first team, the trust of the changing room and captain Ben Clarke's confidence.

Pichot was handed the captaincy for a match later that season, the first for an Argentine in England.

'Challenge'

WHEN JOSÉ LUIS Imhoff replaced Petra as Pumas head coach he told Pichot: 'With me you're going to play better than ever. Let go and play, but be careful because the rest won't go at your rhythm. That'll be the great challenge.'

This was when former All Blacks coach Alex Wyllie came on board as a consultant. He would have a big influence on Pichot's early career and Argentina's World Cup breakthrough in 1999.

Pichot, unorthodox and outspoken, met with opposition even sometimes from within his own first club, CASI, from the beginning of his career. Such adversity steeled him for his achievements later in his career.

His ideas of the need for Pumas players' expenses developed quickly when he saw the difficulties faced by those who came from far-flung provinces like Tucumán, Mendoza and Córdoba, hundreds of miles from Buenos Aires, very much a minority until well into the new millennium, who had to pay their own way.

He finally made his World Cup bow against Wales in the opening match of the 1999 tournament. Richmond had fallen into administration and he was on the verge of joining Bristol under Australia's 1991 World Cup-winning coach Bob Dwyer.

Dwyer said: 'His mind is never still for very long and that is what makes him such a fantastic player. He's very elusive and I'm sure even he doesn't know his next step, that's the essence of the Pumas' game.'

Pichot was a key member of that Pumas team, who lost 23–18 to the hosts but won their other pool games against Samoa and Japan and then upset Ireland 28–24 in a play-off in Lens for a quarter-final place in Dublin where they went out 47–26 to France.

The victory over Ireland was the spark for the team that scaled the heights of Paris in 2007 reaching the semi-finals after a setback in the 2003 tournament in Australia where they missed out on a quarter-final place after a 16–15 defeat by the Irish.

Pichot began early to try seeking changes in the UAR, some financial support particularly for the amateur players in the squad but also so the team could prepare properly for Test matches against far better trained top-tier sides.

'Like this we're not going to come [to play for the Pumas] any more,' the players threatened after a 93–8 roasting by the far fitter All Blacks on a 1997 tour of New Zealand that Pichot missed through injury.

The game in Argentina remained amateur at club level after 1995 but there were benefits the UAR and advertisers were reaping without anything reaching the players.

Pichot and others like Lisandro Arbizu, who became Argentina's youngest captain at 21 in 1992, met with opposition from people in the UAR hierarchy because of their new professional status. Arbizu had joined Brive in 1997 and helped them reach that year's European Cup final which they lost to Bath.

'In '95 they left me out because of how I am but this time the smart ass, the arrogant one, the one who sold out to professionalism, the capricious kid with long hair is going to do the impossible to shine at a World Cup,' Pichot vowed.

Wyllie came in as an assistant and consultant under coach Imhoff in 1996 but the set-up was not to the liking of amateur lobbyists in the UAR.

A string of poor results against leading teams including rare losses away to Japan and Italy in 1998 and early 1999 led to Imhoff being replaced by Héctor 'Pipo' Méndez to work alongside Wyllie.

The pair did not agree on who should be the first choice scrum-half with Wyllie favouring Pichot, who won his duel with Nicolás Fernández Miranda, and Méndez resigned – for various reasons including being considered number two to Wyllie by the UAR – days before the team were due to leave for Cardiff.

Pichot recounts it in his book: 'Two months before the World Cup, Pipo Méndez seemed to still be fighting to leave me out of the team and that's when Alex Wyllie, an ex-All Black who was working as technical advisor to the Pumas and who was fundamental for the future of Argentine rugby, and especially for me, comes into action. On the tour of Scotland and Ireland prior to that World Cup, when I had to win my place again, Pipo decided to drop me for the second match against Ireland . . . He had told me that we would play a Test each, Nico Fernández Miranda and me.

'At the first match of the tour, already in the stadium, an hour before facing Scotland and in the middle of the Murrayfield pitch, Wyllie approached me. He stands in front of me and says: "Today's an historical day, right? It could be the first time Argentina beat Scotland in Scotland." "Yes, Alex," I say. "Let's hope so." He gave me a strange look, as if something was bothering him. "Alex, is there something wrong?" "Look, Agustín, the coaches don't like you. I told them that if they didn't put you in today, I was leaving . . . So better if you play like you've never done before." He gave me a pat, curt like he is, and went off. That chat left me very angry, asking myself again what I'd done wrong. But there was no time to grumble, I had the arena, my place to show myself and in an hour I'd make it mine. Finally we made history, we beat Scotland 31–22 on an afternoon when Octavio Bartolucci shone, a friend who started out together with me. It was memorable and I felt happy for him and for myself. A new story was being written.

'It still seemed strange to me that it had been Alex, someone who was not of the Pumas milieu, who most defended me. I had never received a show of affection from him but the guy was convinced I deserved a place and he'd gone out to support me for sporting ethics . . .

'The pressure exerted by Wyllie for me to be first choice led to Pipo having no better idea than to tell us, Nico and me, that we would play a match each. But after the Test with the Scots, no one thought he would go and change the line-up, but he cleaned me out . . .

'This time, Pipo didn't bring me together with Nico again to explain things . . . So in the clash with Ireland I started as reserve for Nico, who didn't have a good game that day. Wyllie continued to apply pressure, I was sent on in the second half and I played the best second half of my life . . .'

Fame

AFTER ARGENTINA HAD broken their quarter-final jinx, Pichot was feted back home as the country's outstanding sports personality of 1999.

He rivalled Argentina's leading footballers in popularity for his speed of thought and daring, always attacking, rather like a Diego Maradona or Ariel Ortega, socks down by his ankles, and he and the team were mobbed at Ezeiza international airport on their return home by hundreds of admirers and autograph seekers.

The Pumas, with Pichot as standard-bearer and chief spokesman, had transcended their relatively small world of a secondary sport in Argentina.

Pichot pushed for better terms for the players, especially the amateurs based in Argentina. He believed that only with a tightly unified team could the Pumas reach their true potential.

'What we had achieved came on the field of play and that was my main source of pride . . . [and] our best tool for our fight [for better terms],' Pichot wrote in his book.

However, Pichot later admitted that the progress the Pumas had made off the field in terms of their public image had gone too fast and split the squad into the older generation and the younger ones.

This split contributed to their elimination at the pool stage in

Australia in 2003, a bitter blow that could have torn Pichot and Marcelo Loffreda apart.

The coach and his captain had their differences over team selection during the tournament and Loffreda was unhappy with an interview Pichot gave back in Buenos Aires in which he said the team had flopped.

The huge disappointment felt by the team in Australia could have ended their dream but instead it galvanised Loffreda, Pichot and one of the best generations of Argentine players.

'We deserve a second chance,' Pichot told Loffreda in a meeting the pair arranged in March 2004 to find a common way forward. '[We've had] enough of thinking of losing with dignity or by very little.'

Hardly surprisingly, there were hiccups on the way to France 2007, too.

Alejandro Risler was voted chairman of the UAR towards the end of 2005 for the 2006/07 season and with him as secretary Ruso Sanz, who always found ways to flex his muscles in the running of the game in Argentina and get on the wrong side of his perceived rivals.

Sanz wanted influence over the national team and their coaches and there was a rumour that he was looking to get rid of Loffreda, having removed the team manager as soon as he and Risler took office, a move that did not please the squad.

Argentina went on a tour of Europe in November 2005 during which they beat Scotland at Murrayfield and Italy in Genoa. An excited Pichot declared that the team needed to start getting accustomed to winning and be strong off the pitch too for the battles ahead with the UAR.

Soon after, a row broke out over expenses the UAR owed the team, money earned through advertising which had been going into the Puma Fund used mainly to pay bonuses to the home-based amateur players.

It boiled over when Sanz spoke out against the professional players in the squad in an interview in Buenos Aires in 2006.

Sanz's comments received widespread media coverage in France where the majority of Argentina's professionals were playing their club rugby and they responded with an angry open letter to clubs in France and Argentina explaining their position.

This is when the senior players created the Big Six – Pichot and five sort of vice-captains who would each lead a cell of players keeping them informed of team issues.

The row continued and so the players en masse sent a letter to the UAR board resigning from the Pumas. The UAR reacted by sending Ricardo Handley, national teams manager, to Paris to negotiate with the players.

Gato Handley, one of the 1965 tourists to South Africa, realised how serious the players were about their stand against the UAR in their bid to improve how the Pumas were funded and trained.

He told the players they would have their demands met in a week and the squad lifted their resignation threat but when Sanz, who had been away in Germany at the FIFA World Cup, returned to Buenos Aires firm in his opposition to the deal negotiated in Paris, Handley resigned.

'I was against professional rugby to start off with,' Handley said. 'I believe in amateur rugby, but the players convinced me that if the union wants us to play against those [top] teams we have to have similar conditions in terms of training. I agreed with them and I saw the way they trained and the spirit they had. It was a great group of players and I supported them because I thought they were right.'

While Sanz had been away in June 2006, the Pumas appeared reinvigorated by their stand for their rights, winning a home series against Wales (27–25 and 45–27) and narrowly losing to New Zealand (25–19).

With the World Cup less than a year away, the rift remained but performances improved even more in the November Test window. Argentina beat England 25–18 for the first time at Twickenham, a demonstration of the team's new-found inner strength, and Italy 23–16 in Rome before a 27–26 loss to France at Saint-Denis.

Pichot, who by then was playing for Stade Français, spoke to the teams and 300 guests at the post-match dinner at Twickenham, telling them how significant the victory over the inventors of the game at rugby's headquarters was and what it meant to Argentines and to him in particular having lived for five years half a mile from the stadium, closing a circle in which he had 'come, played, grown and won here'.

By the time the Pumas upset hosts France 17–12 in the opening match of the 2007 tournament, about 15 players in the squad were professionals playing in the French Top 14 and English Premiership.

When they faced Ireland in their last pool match at the Parc des Princes a draw would have been enough to reach the quarter-finals but they were mentally attuned to achieving something big while Ireland needed four tries and an eight-point winning margin to reach the last eight.

Pichot saw that match, by then a classic World Cup rivalry, as more important than the shock victory over France in the inaugural match because it would see the Pumas qualify in a way that no one could have predicted before the tournament: as pool winners.

'We've always been very clear about who we are and what we want . . . what's happening is in many ways strange. Argentina are not the most technical team in the world nor do we have the best players. There is more of a psychological explanation,' Pichot told reporters on the eve of the match.

He said the building blocks were talent, hard work and professional dedication, always improving over the eight years of Marcelo Loffreda's tenure as head coach, improving to the point where 'tactically, the first half against France was the best we played in the last eight years.

'There are many things we lack as a team, technically, tactically, but we have other attributes, like a tremendous will to work and a great inspiration to push ourselves, which replaces other things when we come up against rivals better than us.

'That's the soul, the spirit of this team. It's nothing tangible, like some result or other, but rather the conviction of what we want . . . which is very difficult to achieve as a squad and that is in many ways down to the staff.

'This team is committed to a dream . . . We didn't just come to the World Cup and suddenly find ourselves in this situation. No, this team did all this to be able to dream.'

A quarter-final win over Scotland put the Pumas in a semi-final against South Africa which they lost but, putting that disappointment behind them, they beat France again for third place.

In a typically passionate motivational speech by a Pumas captain to his team oozing pride in their sky blue and white shirts before they went out on to the Parc des Princes pitch for the bronze medal match, Pichot shouted: 'This is more than a sports shirt. This is our family, our club, our friends. This is our history; this is ours! What we've done during the last month, the last three months, the last eight or ten years. It's the one we live in, the one we sweat in, the one we cry over, the one we laugh with. It's this one! So, in these 80 minutes let's not have anything left, nothing left! Because now we are really going to play for our history, for the player who's beside you . . . And let's enjoy it, because maybe, and almost certainly, for many of us it will be the last . . . Let's go!'

Pichot was as much a leader off the field as on it and after the bronze medal, he put his mind to obtaining what Argentina had needed for a long time – a place in a top annual international competition.

He retired from Test rugby at 30 when he could have carried on playing and perhaps played at another World Cup in 2011, but he felt a duty to his sport. 'I decided for nearly ten years of my life to give my time to changing the [game's] systems so they were fairer in my country and the world.'

It would take five years of negotiations before Argentina were included in the southern hemisphere's big tournament, the Tri-Nations renamed as the Rugby Championship, in 2012.

Four years later, Argentina entered Super Rugby with the Jaguares franchise, the country's first professional team.

Pichot went on to become vice-chairman to chairman Bill Beaumont at World Rugby in 2016 and then lost the vote for chairman, running against Beaumont on a ticket for change, in 2020 and walked away.

Pichot said if he had been motivated by power he would have simply spent another four years as vice-chairman of World Rugby, waiting for his turn to take the top chair, but becoming a director had been a commitment.

'I no longer have a part in decision-making in international or domestic rugby. I train the under-18s at CASI, that's my passion, the thread I keep with rugby, at the club with my friends from the gang of '74,' he said referring to the 1974 generation he grew up with.

The leader and the magician

ARGENTINA FIELDED JUAN Martín Hernández at fly-half against France in the opening match of the 2007 World Cup with Felipe Contepomi, one of their usual number 10s, at inside centre, and embarked on an impressive run to the bronze medal.

'El Mago' (the magician) had started only once at fly-half for Argentina, against Italy in 2005, in his previous 21 Tests. Usually their full back, he had also not played for the Pumas since a 27–26 loss to France in Paris ten months earlier.

Hernández did not play in Argentina's warm-up against Wales, a 27–20 defeat in Cardiff three weeks before the tournament kicked off in which Federico 'Ninja' Todeschini was the fly-half.

So, how did a previously untested Pumas midfield, parts of which had worked so well for Stade Français in their French championship victory a few months earlier, take the tournament hosts by surprise in their own backyard?

'I'll tell you how it was,' Agustín Pichot told me 14 years later. 'Just as with Felipe, Juani (pronounced Huanee) and I began what was not only a great friendship but also a kind of camaraderie of the game.'

In 2003, Pichot, following four seasons at Bristol where he partnered Felipe Contepomi at half back, arrived at Stade Français at the same time as Hernández, who was 21 and taking his first steps in professional rugby.

'We felt we were players who could have a telling influence on the game. I saw him like myself, when I was a kid of 21, entering a European club, and also Felipe, and in very important positions.

'Juani started playing on the wing at Stade Français, then full back, and talking with him and training with him, I always believed he had a lot of ability to play in the fly-half position where he had played as a kid.

'There were two problems, first I had to convince Loffreda and then I had to convince Felipe. At that time, Loffreda wanted Todeschini at 10, where he had been playing in our most recent matches, like when we beat England at Twickenham.'

Todeschini started the England match in November 2006 on the bench with Contepomi at fly-half but he came on when centre Gonzalo Tiesi was injured midway through the first half and Contepomi moved to inside centre. Todeschini had a great match scoring all but three of Argentina's points, including an interception try, in a 25–18 victory.

'We got together with Loffreda in March 2007 to kind of plan the year. We at Stade Français had been playing very well getting into the French play-offs with David Skréla at fly-half and Juani at centre or full back.

'So, I said to Tano, "Trust me; let Juani play at fly-half," but he, being more conservative, says, "No, I'm still not sure between Felipe and Todeschini."

'I insisted, "Let's try with the double pivot, Juani and Felipe playing together, you'll see it'll work," but he says, "I've never seen Juan [at 10]."'

Pichot then decided he would take the idea of Hernández at fly-half to Stade Français coach Fabien Galthié and 'that's what ends up happening. We become champions of France with that double pivot system.'

Hernández played at fly-half with Skréla outside him in the deciding matches of the French championship. At the World Cup, Felipe Contepomi lined up outside Hernández with Skréla facing them as France's fly-half.

'I believed Felipe and Juan would give the attack speed and also pause and then there was their defence – they were like a wall.'

Loffreda came round to Pichot's idea during the team's World Cup build-up but kept it quiet when they played Wales in Cardiff and the Belgian Invitation XV in Brussels ahead of the tournament.

'We were resting our first-choice fifteen . . . but the team was already set to play with Juan at 10 and Felipe as inside centre. Tano was convinced.'

Hernández, called the Maradona of rugby for his ball skills, and Contepomi went on to have a brilliant World Cup and were both shortlisted along with South Africa's Bryan Habana, the eventual winner, for the IRB Player of the Year award.

Argentina did suffer a setback in Brussels with injury to number 8 Gonzalo 'Chalo' Longo. Juan Manuel Leguizamón stood in for the inaugural match and the next pool game against Georgia, a 33–3 win.

Longo was eased back against Namibia in a 63–3 rout and was brilliant against Ireland, being voted man of the match in a 30–15 victory.

With the try count two apiece against the Irish, Argentina's forward dominance and a masterclass in kicking from hand by Hernández, including a hat-trick of drop goals, made the difference.

Argentina's second try, that gave them an 18–10 half-time lead, started with Hernández catching his own up-and-under and, as he was falling from a tackle, making a superb backhanded layoff to prop Martín Scelzo. The action launched a counter-attack on the right that ended with Horacio Agulla touching down in the opposite corner.

Longo scored Argentina's try in the 19–13 quarter-final win over Scotland before Argentina's charge through the tournament was halted by South Africa, who won their semi-final 37–13. Hernández, who could drop goals with both feet, got another with his left against the Scots.

Director

PICHOT RECALLED THAT Argentina's build-up to what turned out to be such a good World Cup for the Pumas was, just as in 1999, fraught with problems with the UAR.

'For me it was a learning curve, first as a player, then as a person and afterwards as a director on the pitch, because I felt I was a director while playing.

'It was a lesson in principles, conditions, remaining very solid as a team and as players who had been protagonists, having even to defend our coach, like that time when Pato Noriega appeared in Rome and we told him he shouldn't be at our hotel because we already had coaches, a move to oust or destabilise Tano right after we beat England.

'Tano wanted to resign and I told him not to, [saying] the whole team supported him. That's a very big show of solidarity in a team, of maturity and conviction.

'That has probably happened in very few teams in the world where we came out in defence of the coaching staff. We felt we'd been offended.

'Ruso Sanz, as a member of the UAR leadership, would have been within his rights to announce a change of coach. We players don't appoint or sack the coaches.

'But we felt that ethically it was right to back them and had we ended up not playing it would have been the second time [we had made the threat], not out of spite over bonuses but because we were defending our coach. It was a lack of respect.'

The UAR directors realised in that make-or-break situation that Argentina could end up without their best team at the World Cup if they had persisted in their stance. Instead, they provided Loffreda and the players with the best preparation they had ever had.

'But there were times when I didn't know what the right thing to do was like when José Luis Imhoff was ousted in '99 with some players involved in the move.

'I didn't have the influence [to speak] for the whole team, to say "We're not going there." I didn't have that leadership which I did in 2007.

'So those were two very extreme situations, one which I experienced when I was young, 25 years old and having just lost my dad. It was my first World Cup, I was a bit selfish – "Let the captain sort it" – and I wasn't the captain. Then the other as captain, with all the players' support.' Pichot referred to the 1999 World Cup as his first because in South Africa in 1995 as a 21-year-old he was in the squad but did not play.

Risler, Sanz and Hugo Porta with Handley as team manager had won the 2005 UAR election but after what happened in 2007 'they were very much weakened politically which was a shame because I think Hugo could have done a lot in the international context'.

Summarising his years as a director in Argentine rugby, Pichot said: 'It was a huge amount of work, very intensive, in which we set a very clear north for a federal game in Argentina. We then set about changing the mentality of a centralised game in the world to a more inclusive one so Argentina would have a chance, a fairer place in the game.

'It was a lot of work, by many people; countless trips, lots of convincing people who didn't believe in us.

'That's why it was so satisfying finishing fourth in the 2015 World Cup and reaching a Super Rugby final (in 2019) and that the players should have come from all the provinces was, I think, a great success.'

As vice-chairman of World Rugby from 2016 to 2020, Pichot sought stiffer eligibility rules than three-year residency for players hopeful of playing international rugby in their adopted countries.

'I've never liked it and I don't like it now, that the most powerful countries use their economies or make rules to weaken the weaker teams, inviting players to play in their countries, seducing them when they're young.

'It's great that the Fijians, Tongans, Argentines play in the European clubs and earn money but I don't think Italy, England, Ireland, Scotland, Wales, France, New Zealand or Australia should profit from that, which they've been doing for the last 30 years.

'I don't think it's right to limit players' options to play for their country because they earn more money [abroad] than playing for Fiji. It weakens the development of Fiji, who could have an incredible team.'

Pichot resigned from the World Rugby council and Rugby Americas presidency when he lost his bid to win the top job in the game and said he would only consider another shot at the chairmanship if he had something to offer.

'I am more and more sceptical as I look at it from the outside. Yes, if I had something to contribute, but for now I see that I have nothing to contribute. They are all returning favours; it's all much darker than I thought. What we were fighting for, now they are fixing with favours, tours; it's a real shame.'

TWENTY

LEICESTER

IT IS LATE in October 2007 in Leicester when Marcelo Loffreda stands in front of his players for the first time, among them some England internationals like Ben Kay and Lewis Moody who have just returned from the World Cup in France where they lost to South Africa in the final.

Also present at Leicester Tigers' Welford Road ground are Ireland full back Geordan Murphy and Scotland lock Jim Hamilton, whose teams were beaten by Argentina as Loffreda steered his Pumas to third place in the tournament.

Perhaps this date is part of the problem Loffreda faces taking charge of the Tigers because he has missed the pre-season and early Premiership fixtures that would have helped him settle into the task.

The season had opened on 15 September, a week after the World Cup had kicked off with Argentina's shock win over hosts France in the opening match. Loffreda was engaged throughout the tournament as the Pumas reached and won the bronze medal match, also against France on 20 October.

Most of these Leicester players are completely new to him, apart from Argentina prop Marcos Ayerza, regardless of whether some faced his Pumas playing for rival nations in Test matches.

Loffreda is suddenly alone, a man who won the admiration of the rugby world for the way he marshalled the Pumas into a side that was one defeat from reaching the World Cup final, whose players were close, some younger ones surrogate sons, the coaching staff much more his friends than colleagues.

He must have been a very good coach to have persuaded one of England's top clubs to take him on with a view perhaps to giving them something new and different while keeping them at the top of one of the world's major professional club championships and getting paid for the first time in his life at 48 for doing such a job.

This is a long way from the Argentine amateur rugby environment where he had spent almost his entire life, a world of family, friends, club teammates, and at international level always betting against the odds and sometimes overcoming them.

After his playing career, coaching followed automatically, first at San Isidro Club, then the Buenos Aires representative team, then the Pumas, then all three at the same time for a few months before deciding he should concentrate only on the national side.

All the while Loffreda, a civil engineer, was doing his job as sales manager at Alpargatas, a leading Argentine textile company.

And all of this is normal, the life of an amateur rugby man in Argentina, a life of sharing club relationships, friendships and solidarity while a select minority become good enough to represent them all in Tests against the world's best.

Walking into Leicester like that is not normal, even less so alone without his own coaching staff . . . but he has earned this chance to test himself in an altogether different, demanding environment.

He still represents his club SIC, his city Buenos Aires, his country Argentina and the fact that he lasts a single season is not a failure, quite the contrary given that the Tigers reach two finals and many people involved with them are sad to see him go back to a world he fits better after 'an enriching experience'.

This is the same English club that tried and failed to lure his Pumas captain Agustín Pichot from Richmond ten years earlier before the pair were to embark on their incredible, roller-coaster World Cup journey.

It was also in the same country where eight years later, the Pumas would reach the World Cup semi-finals for the second time – and the same city that became a home from home where they won two pool matches – with a side that Pichot had installed in an annual elite international tournament, the southern hemisphere's Rugby Championship, where it could put behind it decades of limited competition to earn full recognition of its place in the top ten.

'I hadn't imagined my future linked permanently and professionally to rugby. I had my profession and my job.

'When I went to Leicester I saw that at least for a time I could transform myself into a rugby professional but not for ever; that was never my idea.

'Now look how things have turned out that practically my main job is in rugby because I became coordinator and games director for the Buenos Aires provincial union, URBA.' This was in 2013 before returning in 2020 to the Pumas as their manager.

Loffreda was recommended to Leicester by their former fly-half Les Cusworth, who had played for the Tigers with their chief executive Peter Wheeler during the most successful years of their club and international careers in the late '70s and 1980s. 'I recommended Marcelo to Peter Wheeler, the CEO of Leicester Tigers – Peter and I played together and worked together in an insurance brokerage as directors for many years – on the basis of what he'd done for Argentina over the seven years, the most successful Argentine rugby coach ever.

'I saw his strengths with management and dealing with people and I thought he'd be great as a director of rugby for Leicester Tigers so Marcelo was interviewed by the board and Peter Wheeler in Leicester and they liked what they saw.

'Marcelo is a wonderful rugby man, a man of great integrity and we felt that he could do a good job for Leicester.

'When he arrived at Leicester the club was in transition, and the elder statesmen among the players were looking at coaching careers. It was literally a changing of the guard at Leicester, not an easy environment for Marcelo to get involved in.

'Marcelo went over on his own with a very successful track record and, I think it's fair to say, he got a young coaching group he tried to pull together, some ambitious young men, and it was not easy to manage.

'And Leicester were used to winning, not coming second, and the Argentine, and Marcelo's, management style, maybe in hindsight, was not quite right for Leicester at that time.

'They had a very in-your-face attitude with players and a very hard line that brought a lot of success to the Tigers in the 1990s with that approach, with Martin Johnson, Dean Richards and others. It was a well-oiled machine.

'It didn't quite work out for him but it didn't diminish Marcelo in any way, him as a manager, him as a person.'

Loffreda said that in retrospect he would have changed aspects of his work at Leicester having gone there with a strictly amateur mentality despite having trained the Argentine national team for many years.

'I would probably have named assistants who were close to me, in whom I had maximum confidence and not gone alone, completely unprotected, to an environment I didn't know.

'I would also have arranged with the people at Leicester to be granted a certain amount of time to adapt to such a different regime.

'One thing is to coach a national team and another is a club, where you are all day without interruption and which consumes you and you have to resolve issues without a breather because the next weekend you have to play another match, and the more so given it's the Premiership.

'On the one hand it was really good because it was an education

– though with some blows. I don't regret it at all because it was a great experience, but it was very hard as a family because we all went there, we all had to adapt, but it was enriching.'

Loffreda, who had gone to England with his wife and five children, was sacked after the end of the season, in June 2008, the bottom line being that they did not win any trophies.

'They were unsparing in that we played three championships and lost two finals; it wasn't a catastrophe, we weren't relegated, but clearly the results were the decisive factor.'

Fans were generally very supportive of Loffreda and he was shown lots of online chats expressing support for him, added to which he was a friend of Cusworth, whom he describes as 'a Leicester man through and through even though he wasn't living there'.

'You could say I was frustrated because during the short time I was there I never managed to adapt. Then I also made mistakes, of course, like going alone with no trusted aide to a place where everything worked, everything was super professional, there were coaches who had been there for quite some time.

'I was also indirectly in charge of the Leicester academy, so there were lots of new things and I assumed I would adapt much more easily and that didn't happen and in that sense I think I made a mistake in not asking for more help.'

When Loffreda took charge at Leicester there were three Argentine-born front-row players in the squad: Ayerza, Italy prop Martin Castrogiovanni and Alejandro Moreno, who won a handful of caps playing for Argentina and then Italy.

Ayerza, who played at three World Cups, spent a decade at Welford Road making 246 appearances and played against his club and for the Pumas in his testimonial match, which doubled as a warm-up for the 2015 World Cup. It was the second time Argentina had faced Leicester, having also played a World Cup warm-up there in 2007.

Cusworth recalls Ayerza asking him early in his Pumas career in 2005: 'Do you know a club called Leicester?'

'I said, well, yes, I spent a few years there and played a few games for them . . . It's been an ongoing joke between us for the last 15 years.'

Other Argentines to have played for Leicester include wings Horacio Agulla and Gonzalo Camacho and flanker Pablo Matera.

There were four Argentines in the squad in the 2020/21 season: forwards Tomás Lavanini and Julián Montoya and backs Matías Moroni and Joaquín Díaz Bonilla who joined after Super Rugby was suspended due to Covid-19 and the Jaguares were disbanded for lack of a competition.

TWENTY-ONE

LES

ARGENTINA OWES A debt of gratitude to Rugby School, where the game was born 200 years ago, for the cameo role played by the late chairman of governors, Sir Ewen Fergusson, at the turn of this century in the Pumas' climb to the 2007 World Cup podium.

Former Leicester Tigers and England fly-half Les Cusworth was working for Rugby School Enterprises Limited when in 2000, at the start of Marcelo Loffreda's tenure as Argentina's head coach, he was asked by the national union UAR to become an advisor to the Pumas.

Cusworth had already been a regular visitor to Argentina, where his second wife is from, giving free clinics at the UAR, the Buenos Aires provincial union URBA and clubs while he was director of rugby at Worcester RC in the late 1990s.

Over tea and scones at his mother-in-law's home in the Hurlingham suburb where Cusworth now lives, the UAR's director of national teams Emilio 'Gringo' Perasso, accompanied by Loffreda, said he would like Cusworth to be technical advisor to the Pumas and the contract would be '*corazón y pasión*'.

Cusworth's wife was acting as interpreter so when she went into the kitchen for more tea he followed. 'I asked my wife, "What are they saying?" and she said, "There is no contract, you'd be working for heart and passion," the symbols of Argentine rugby.

'Back at Rugby, I went to see Sir Ewen, the chairman of governors and a career diplomat, who was my boss along with headmaster Patrick Derham and said I'd been approached by the UAR to be a technical advisor to the Pumas on an honorary basis.'

Fergusson, who was capped by Scotland five times as a lock in 1954, replied: 'All I can say, Les, is thank God amateur rugby is alive and kicking. You've got my absolute total support and Patrick Derham has agreed with me; we think it's wonderful for rugby, wonderful for our institution, wonderful for everybody. What we'll do is we'll give you four more weeks' paid holiday to go and do it for them.'

'I started in November 2001 when Argentina toured Scotland and Wales. I spent a week with them in Cardiff, where they beat Wales comfortably (30–16). I didn't go to Scotland where they also won (25–16).

'Being in the middle of it, you realise these people have got something very special, their pride and passion, sacrifice and commitment. That was my first real taste; young Contepomi, young Pichot, young men playing like they were seasoned campaigners, Arbizu, Omar Hasan; all the players were all so welcoming, to an outsider really, coming in to help them.

'I can't speak more highly of them. If anything shows the values of amateur rugby and what club rugby provides in Argentina it's exactly that: the values in the behaviour of the players.'

The following month, Cusworth's next assignment was a Test match at the River Plate stadium in Buenos Aires against New Zealand when the Pumas came within a whisker of a first victory over the All Blacks.

'A week before I was due to fly to Buenos Aires to help Marcelo in that game I got a telephone call from the UAR: would I please collect the match balls from Gilbert Rugby Balls, who were based in Rugby.

'They were black balls specifically for that game and specifically for the high-performance internationals. How many unions have the balls delivered just a week before an international? That just showed Argentina for the uniqueness it has in world rugby. It certainly is a unique rugby nation and one that people should admire greatly.'

Early contact

CUSWORTH, WHO WON 12 caps, crossed paths with Argentine rugby in a variety of places before becoming directly involved with the Pumas, starting with a tour match in 1978 prior to Argentina's 13–13 draw with England at Twickenham in the countries' first meeting.

That first contact was playing for North Midlands, the county champions, at Moseley, the club he was playing for at the time. The Pumas won 22–14.

'It was a fearsome, physical game of rugby. There was very little expansive rugby; it was the first time I saw at first hand the real power of the Argentine forwards and the passion and the commitment they played with.'

A player from each side, number 8 Derek Nutt and scrum-half Alfredo Soares Gache, were sent off for fighting near the end, which meant the Argentine missed the game with England.

Cusworth won his first cap against New Zealand a year later, having joined Leicester Tigers.

Then in 1981, Cusworth and Leicester teammates Peter Wheeler and Clive Woodward played for the Barbarians at the Hong Kong Sevens, which they won after a narrow quarter-final win (8–6) over an Argentine side that included Hugo Porta, Loffreda and Daniel Baetti making their first appearance in an international sevens tournament and learning on the go.

A decade passed during which there was no rugby contact with Argentina after the Malvinas/Falklands War.

'I coached England Students and in 1992 we played at the Student World Cup in Italy. England had some fantastic backs and who should we get in our group in Sardinia but Argentina, a team thrown together because they didn't have finances to plan or do anything properly.

'We prepared for four months, we were going to play a really expansive game and run them off the park . . . and we got absolutely murdered in the scrum and lost.

'That was a real wake-up call for me in my coaching. You can talk about all the planning, strategy, how you're going to use the ball, but if you don't get the ball in the first place, you don't have the forwards to do it, everything else goes out of the window.

'That was a clear message to me about the importance of forwards and the dark arts of rugby and the set piece. They clearly showed that in order to win matches at that level you need heart, passion and commitment that Argentina are never short of.'

Prop Omar Hasan, a member of the 2007 World Cup bronze medal team, was one of a handful of players in that Argentine students' side who would go on to play for the Pumas.

The following year, Cusworth coached the England team to victory in the first Sevens World Cup in Edinburgh.

'Outside Murrayfield stadium afterwards, four big Argentines, including Raúl Sanz and Alejandro Risler, stopped me and said they wanted to invite us to the Punta del Este Sevens in Uruguay in January 1994. I said, "I'm going off to celebrate now," but I scribbled my number on a piece of paper for them and a month later I got an official invitation to Uruguay . . . And that's where I met my wife.'

Pointers

CUSWORTH SINGLES OUT some Tests played during his

periodic get-togethers with the Pumas between 2001 and 2006 that were indicative of what they could achieve.

'There were some games which made you think we could do really well in 2007.'

In November 2004, Argentina played France in Marseille and won 24–14, a huge upset against the reigning Six Nations Grand Slam champions that ended their eight-match unbeaten run that year.

'It was a real message to me, and I've been in rugby a long, long time but my God this country's got something special; it's built to compete and win and they did it with some cracking rugby. The strength of character of some of the players, they are incredible rugby people – that was a real show of the strength of rugby in Argentina.'

The next was the 25–25 draw with the British and Irish Lions in Cardiff in May 2005 when, due to Rule 9, Argentina were short of 26 players yet were only deprived of victory by a Jonny Wilkinson penalty in injury time.

'The first training session was not very good, a group of total strangers, and within five or six days the coaches got them all together thinking they could take on the British Lions.

'I said to Loffreda, "Tano, this is going to be 80 points," but I had totally underestimated the passion and belief these guys have and they got within a whisker of beating the Lions.'

Then in June 2006 there was a two-Test series at home to Wales and Argentina took them down to Patagonia for the first meeting at Puerto Madryn, in territory that was colonised by Welsh settlers in 1865.

'Wales came over and we played them down by Trelew of all places. I said to the UAR, "Why are we doing this?" and they said, "Oh, we thought they would like it, it will be great for the community and a great fillip for rugby in that area and the people in that area."

'Typical of Argentina and totally unselfish, the UAR took Wales to the home of Wales to play a key game. They didn't think of the ramifications of the team running out to a sea of red and the Wales team being announced to a chorus of typical Welsh songs, you know, "Land of my Fathers" and all that.

'I said to Loffreda, "I thought this was supposed to be a home game," and we burst out laughing. But we won the game (27–25) and Argentina won the series (45–27 in the second Test) a week later in Buenos Aires.

'The big game was probably Argentina beating England (25–18) in 2006, a game against a star-studded team, star-studded coaching bench, in a full house at Twickenham, Argentina totally unprepared as such because of their commitments.

'Those four games were an enormous message for me in the last 50 years of rugby that I've been involved in with Leicester, England and Argentina.

'So coming into 2007, everything was geared towards them doing really well and there was a lot of difficulty with professional and amateur rugby at the time so you've got to give credit to the union and also the strength of character of the players and coaches for what they did, a really heart-warming moment about what the real values of rugby are.

'Everybody was so confident we could get a result in our favour in that first game but if you look at the reality of rugby everything was stacked in favour of France.

'After the game, the look of shock on [Bernard] Laporte's face – he was coaching France – because it was all geared up to be France's party and 35, 40 coaches and players from Argentina totally ruined the party.

'It was a real pleasure to be a small part of it.'

Argentina were up against France again in the third-place play-off following the disappointment of losing their semi-final to South Africa.

Cusworth compared Argentina's response in the bronze medal match with England's in 1995. 'I was assistant coach with England in South Africa when we lost to New Zealand in the semi-final.

'My recollection of that, England playing France in the third and fourth play-off, was that the players had lost their mojo, if you like, lost their goal of winning the big prize and it was a game they really didn't want to play.

'Turn to twelve years later in France, the Pumas have had the real downer of losing the semi-final to South Africa, but the game for third and fourth place was an enormous game for Argentina.

'Argentina played some fantastic rugby. People say they played limited rugby, but when you look back on those years Loffreda had the Pumas in his hands, they played some tremendous rugby.

'The founding clubs are more than 150 years old and people don't realise how long they've been going here and the strength of rugby in Argentina and how it's managed to maintain the real values of the game: the sacrifice, the giving, learning and helping each other – it's an example of what rugby is all about.'

High performance

IN 2004, TIER One funding became available for the top ten nations in the world from the IRB (International Rugby Board), now World Rugby. 'At that stage I think that was about US$2 million over three years, and Argentina had been fighting for Tier One status.'

When the world rankings were introduced in 2003, Argentina were ranked seventh. They reached a record highest position of third after they won the bronze medal at the 2007 World Cup in France.

'The funding was for high performance, to basically look after the elite to play international rugby. It was taking players out of clubs all around the world to fund international teams and not the base of the game.

'There were two years of discussions, no agreement and Argentina got nothing. In the end the UAR realised there had to be compromise.

'The IRB suggested to the UAR, "Why don't we propose Les Cusworth becomes the director of rugby for Argentina to head up the PladAR [*Plan para Desarrollo y Alto Rendimiento* (plan for development and high performance)], working in the middle between Argentina and the IRB."

'In October 2006, they said "We'll give you the funding – it's for high performance and also development."

'It was the only plan in the world at the time integrating high performance and club rugby.

'The IRB said it would never work but they put me in the middle to make sure the money was spent in the right way.

'There was a real reluctance to accept high performance because the protection and integration of amateur rugby in Argentina is paramount.

'To be fair, the UAR were trying to protect amateur rugby and I applaud that.

'My job, working with the officials, was to look at what had been done in other countries – England, Wales, France, New Zealand, South Africa and Australia – and then modify that as appropriate for Argentina, making sure amateur rugby was protected.

'None of them fitted the infrastructure of Argentine rugby so Agustín Pichot came up with the idea of not spending any of the money on infrastructure but to work with the provinces and the municipalities of the areas where we were going to go to use existing facilities, modify them and use the staff where possible, retrain the staff so you minimise the investment and he called them virtual centres – a brilliant idea – using other people's money not your own.

'The plan agreed with the UAR and Mark Egan of the IRB was for five centres in the major rugby-playing provinces [and cities]: Buenos Aires, Córdoba, Tucumán, Mendoza and Rosario . . . Now there are centres dotted all around the country.

'Córdoba were the first to show any sign of interest while other provinces were sort of reticent to be the first to get involved.

'I had a meeting with the province's vice-governor, former basketball international 'Pichi' Campana, and in the first two minutes he said to me, "Les, I want the first centre to be here; what do you require of me?"

'That was a breath of fresh air, totally different to everybody else's approach around the country.'

Córdoba chose their 1978 FIFA World Cup stadium Chateau Carreras, later renamed Mario Kempes, which was in a state of disrepair. 'No investment in the gymnasium, windows smashed, damaged basketball courts, pitches overgrown with grass, everything needed a coat of paint.

'Campana said, "We'll match the investment of the IRB and the UAR. The centre's got to be used both for the community and for the rugby high performance," and it worked brilliantly.

'Clubs decreed that the high-performance sessions would be only for players aged 17 and upwards – they would not want the under-17s involved because they thought it was too early, what with their academic studies. It was by invitation and there were about 40 seniors.'

The Argentina squad, 41 players, had already experienced high-performance preparation for the 2007 World Cup, spending three weeks at the Athletes' Performance facility on the Andrews Institute campus in Pensacola, Florida which, like the Pumas, was sponsored by adidas.

'The improvements in their fitness, especially that of the front five forwards, were especially notable.

'The training methods in Pensacola were incorporated in the PladAR system along with all the training methodology NZ Rugby used: handling, vision, scanning, using your fingers to catch and pass – all the skill elements of all the academies in New Zealand we modified and put into our system.'

Next was Tucumán where a small club, Los Tarcos, was chosen for ease of access in the centre of the provincial capital, San Miguel de Tucumán. 'When we told the president of Los Tarcos, he cried in front of me; he was so proud of what his little club had achieved.

'For the next three years they were the two provinces that really pushed the PladAR out; they won everything . . . and really shocked URBA.'

Between 2009 and 2014 Córdoba, nicknamed 'Los Dogos', and Tucumán, 'La Naranja' (orange), won three titles each in the national inter-province championship.

'This was the direct result of the work managers and staff in those provinces put into their PladAR centres. They did an incredible job with what they had.'

Rosario's Los Ñandúes (rheas) reached three of those finals and Las Aguilas (eagles) of Buenos Aires (URBA) only one before they won the tournament in its last three seasons from 2015 to 2017 after which it was discontinued.

Virreyes

AT THE LOWEST grassroots level of development is the shining example of Virreyes Rugby Club.

Marcos Julianes of Club Atlético San Isidro and Carlos Ramallo of San Isidro Club may have been bitter rivals on the rugby field whenever their teams met in the Buenos Aires suburb's 'clásico', SIC v CASI – but they are best of friends off it.

In a typical progression in Argentine amateur rugby both went on to coach at various levels in their respective clubs before in 2002 they started a new venture to take the game to *villa miseria* (shanty town) kids in the neighbouring suburb of San Fernando.

Their initiative won Virreyes the IRB Spirit of Rugby Award in 2010. The club went on to be supported by the Atlas Foundation, started in 2014 by former England prop Jason Leonard, that sponsors such projects of social inclusion throughout the world.

'The Virreyes club in Buenos Aires were given a merit award by the IRB as an example of what rugby provides for the communities around the world, to reflect the work the club had done – [Rodolfo] O'Reilly and Marcos Julianes and the other founders of Virreyes,' said Cusworth, who is in charge of Atlas's Argentina All Schools programme.

The late coach Rodolfo 'Michingo' O'Reilly, a CASI man, became involved in Virreyes and regarded his work there as more fulfilling than anything he had done before, like coaching the Pumas and being Sports Secretary for the government on the country's return to democracy in 1983. 'We're immersed in something with the basic condiment of love for your neighbour. Argentina needs a lot of this, which is the antidote to violence,' he said in a 2005 interview in the national newspaper *Página/12*.

Virreyes do not just coach rugby for the hundreds of boys and girls who have joined the club but also carry out an integral control of the kids, checking how they are getting on at school, their health and their behaviour in the home, in most cases mere shacks, and outside.

Cusworth added: 'To me Virreyes is a classic example of what rugby means in Argentina, of giving, sacrifice, helping others, making it a game for people of all social backgrounds and the fit was perfect, and for the last five or six years Atlas have continued to support Virreyes in bringing boys and girls from the "villa" in San Fernando.

'And they have also extended their programme into the poor areas of west Buenos Aires and particularly into a project called Rugby in the Barrios in Salta run by Marcelo Córdova, a rugby fanatic who is Sports Secretary of the province.'

Marcelo Loffreda and other former Pumas like Juan 'Chipi' Figallo, who is from Salta in the north-west of Argentina, and Pato Albacete have helped with these projects.

Reaching out

'WE SAY VIRREYES is the extension of the borders of our clubs. We didn't leave; I'm almost a life member of CASI and Carlos of SIC,' says Julianes.

'We have sought the help of our clubs and all the rest of them; we are proud to have come out of our clubs and San Isidro and the clásico to show a way of experiencing sport in Virreyes.'

Julianes played in the front row for CASI in the 1980s at the same time that Ramallo, a wing with SIC, won his three Pumas caps in the South American Championship in Chile in October 1979.

'San Isidro's got that. It's a brotherhood; we're rivals and brothers who when it's time for each of us to go to his club, we go our separate ways and we live it with intensity.

'It's a very special derby; I don't know if there's anything like it anywhere else in the world with that crossed blood and from the same neighbourhood and the affection we have for each other and how alike we are when the match is over.

'The year 2002 was a tough year for Argentina, which was emerging from an almost terminal crisis with an increase in poverty above 50 per cent.'

Julianes and Ramallo and their wives were volunteers at schools in the poor district of Virreyes, a 15-minute drive from San Isidro, helping feed the children at lunchtime.

One day, drinking 'mate' with the head teacher, Carlos wondered out loud what it might be like to introduce the children, whose only likely sport was football, to rugby. 'It seemed a crazy idea at the time.'

But then it dawned on Julianes that so much dedication to rugby during most of his life suddenly made sense in starting something new and revolutionary, 'dedicating ourselves to taking the game to kids who didn't have access to it although we later found that similar initiatives existed with less fanfare in many places.

'Many people joined us: Pumas, coaches, 'Michingo', [the late] Pancho Maggio, who ended up quadriplegic (at 17) playing rugby and he helped coach as much as he could from his wheelchair.

'We created a large community; we say it's everyone's club because all the clubs wanted to come and help.

'And this club works as a place to learn, to get support and to help each other, me included.'

Virreyes has had a senior team from 2010 and they have climbed through three levels of the URBA league system to Primera C, the fourth tier.

It is remarkable to see Virreyes, born from a shanty town in 2003, on a fixture list that includes Old Georgian, founded in 1908 by the old boys of the Anglo-Argentine St George's School, modelled on British public schools such as Rugby.

TWENTY-TWO

IRB

THE 2003 WORLD Cup in Australia highlighted an issue of great concern for the IRB (World Rugby from 2014): teams sometimes being hammered by more than 100 points in their games against elite nations eight years into the open professional era.

This did not directly concern Argentina. They had already bounced back from their worst ever Test defeat, 93–8 against the All Blacks in New Zealand in 1997, two years before their World Cup breakthrough into the best eight.

But the IRB played a key part in Argentina becoming regularly competitive with the top European and southern hemisphere teams, helping the UAR set up their high-performance centres and find a place in an annual elite international tournament.

Mark Egan, who as World Rugby's Head of Competitions and Performance drove the programme to give the second-tier nations a better chance of competing with the elite, spoke highly of Argentina's progress during the 2015 World Cup in England.

'Argentina are a unique example. They were always very strong internationally, with a long history in the game; a very strong rugby structure in the country where rugby is perceived as a very strong sport with over 600 clubs and over 100,000 players. They have been a force on the international stage for many years,' Egan said.

'The key decision was that Argentina's future was in the southern hemisphere, not northern, and that they should be included in the Rugby Championship and that Regulation Nine should apply to them when they were in the Rugby Championship.'

Regulation Nine obliged clubs to release their international players, something that had historically been a problem for Argentina outside the traditional Test windows in June and November, for example the Pumas' match against the British and Irish Lions in Cardiff in May 2005.

Argentina had gradually more and more of their internationals playing for clubs in England, France and Ireland after the turn of the century. The Rugby Championship they joined in 2012 is played between August and early October during the early part of the European season.

'The Sanzar unions (Australia, New Zealand and South Africa) opened their doors to Argentina and it was important to know Argentina had the playing base and structure to become competitive within the championship,' Egan continued. With Argentina's inclusion, the group became Sanzaar.

'The [Argentine] union itself went through some tremendous transformation in governance structure and the implementation of the PladAR, the regional high-performance training centres.

'It was a very well-thought-out strategy and Gus Pichot was very much at the forefront and lobbying that and now they are in Super Rugby. They had very strong foundations and a proven track record at international level against Tier One nations, it was a very important decision for World Rugby and Sanzar to bring them in. It's great to see that 25 of the [Pumas] players at this (2015) World Cup have come through that.'

The creation of the Jaguares franchise to play in Super Rugby from 2016 ensured that a small nucleus of professional players contracted to the UAR were playing at home in line with the southern hemisphere calendar.

'This investment programme has been going on for eight years and we're seeing the fruits now. This World Cup has shown us that high performance is not like a tap; you can't turn it on and off, it's a long-term investment. It's a bit like preparing an Olympic athlete so it's a really holistic view that we take with each union; there are different needs and wants.

'We spend £8 million a year on development and £10 million on high performance and I look after the high-performance programme and the competitions programme. The money comes from the Rugby World Cup and when the exco made the decision in 2006 to spend £10 million a year we didn't necessarily have the money to do it; we've basically been spending ahead of ourselves but we have been spending the profits from this World Cup over the last eight years so we work in four-year cycles.

'This World Cup has been very successful commercially but we've already been spending the money ahead of ourselves because we had to do something in 2006. We had some very poor results in 2003; Australia beat Namibia by over 140 points, we had big scores, 80 plus, 90 plus against Tier Two unions.

'We said we have to protect the integrity of the tournament, we have to help the Tier Two unions and we need to spend money to do that so it's been our investment, but also the unions saw that World Rugby was coming in to help not only with money but also expertise.'

At the 1999 World Cup, New Zealand beat Italy 101–3 and England beat Tonga 101–10. In 2003, hosts Australia beat Romania 90–8 and then Namibia 142–0, England beat Georgia 84–6 and Uruguay 111–13.

In 2007, Australia beat Japan 91–3 and New Zealand beat Portugal 108–13. In 2011, South Africa beat Japan 87–0 but in 2015 the Japanese upset the Springboks 34–32 and the biggest winning margin was South Africa's 64–0 win over the United States. Argentina's biggest loss at a World Cup was 46–15 to New Zealand in 1987.

TWENTY-THREE

RUGBY CHAMPIONSHIP

———————— 🐾 ————————

SANTIAGO PHELAN REMAINED a staunch amateur throughout his playing career as a flanker for CASI and Argentina, including two World Cups in 1999 and 2003, then cut his coaching teeth with his beloved club before taking over from Loffreda as Pumas head coach in 2008.

He became only the second man and first Argentine to be paid as Pumas coach after New Zealander Alex Wyllie.

Phelan's Pumas side did as well as could be expected at the next World Cup in New Zealand in 2011.

They lost 13–9 to England in their opening pool match but a 13–12 victory over Scotland in Wellington with a rousing try by Lucas González Amorosino ensured they reached a quarter-final against the All Blacks, which they lost 33–10.

The win against Scotland was not altogether unexpected since Phelan's side had beaten the Scots twice in five previous meetings since 2008.

Phelan had enjoyed a winning start at the helm with a 21–15 victory over Scotland in Rosario in June 2008 but had to settle for a drawn series after losing the second Test 26–14 in Buenos Aires.

It was the beginning of a long and hard road with a team in transition after the retirement of key members of the 2007 bronze medal Pumas like scrum-half Agustín Pichot, full back Nani Corleto, number 8 Gonzalo Longo, lock Nacho Fernández Lobbe and prop Omar Hasan.

More defeats followed, a surprise 13–12 upset at home to Italy and a crushing 63–9 rout in South Africa in an August Test match celebrating Nelson Mandela's 90th birthday with the Pumas largely made up of players not fully fit and off the pace in the European pre-season.

A key element of ill-prepared Pumas sides in the days when they lacked an annual international tournament and could count on only six matches per year in the June and November Test windows was staying strong for the full 80 minutes against top opposition.

The game against the reigning world champions in Johannesburg was a case in point with the Pumas running up a 9–0 lead in the opening half hour from penalties kicked by Felipe Contepomi before the South Africans, who went 14–9 up before half-time, ran riot totalling nine converted tries.

For their November tour of Europe, Argentina hired Frenchman Fabien Galthié as a technical advisor to Phelan. The Pumas beat Italy between defeats in France and Ireland.

In June 2009, the UAR were granted a request to stage the first Test of a home series against England at Old Trafford to generate much-needed funds and lost 37–15 before winning the second Test 24–22 in Salta. That November they lost a two-Test series in Wales before beating Scotland 9–6 at Murrayfield.

The following year also began against Scotland but with Argentina losing a home series 2–0 before they closed out the Test window with a 41–13 victory over France in Buenos Aires with captain Felipe Contepomi notching 31 points including two tries.

On tour in November they beat Italy before losing to France and Ireland then warmed up for the World Cup with a 28–13 loss to Wales in Cardiff in August 2011, their only Test that year against a leading rugby nation outside of the tournament in New Zealand.

While Phelan was presiding over the Pumas' transition from the Loffreda era, Pichot was busy fulfilling his dream of finding Argentina a place in an annual international competition.

Argentina's progress in international rugby had been driven by the players, with Pichot as standard-bearer, pushing the UAR for more help in making the Pumas competitive.

The IRB, acutely aware of the huge gap between the leading nations and the other teams making up the numbers at World Cups, set aside funds to help countries including Argentina develop their international players.

Having retired from Test rugby, although he still played at club level in France until 2009, Pichot's talks with the IRB and Sanzar, the body running the southern hemisphere's Tri-Nations tournament, took five years to bear fruit. When Argentina's entry to the Rugby Championship was confirmed, the organisation's name was tweaked to Sanzaar.

Argentina made their debut as the fourth team in the newly constituted Rugby Championship on 18 August 2012 after a June Test window at home that yielded a 37–22 win over Italy in San Juan and a shared series with France.

The UAR recruited World Cup-winning coach Graham Henry as a consultant to help Phelan but life became tougher for the Pumas as underdogs in all their encounters with New Zealand, South Africa and Australia.

Long-distance travel became another telling element the Argentines had to get used to as they crossed the Pacific Ocean for away games against the All Blacks and Wallabies before seeing out the tournament at home to both.

Having lost their first match away to South Africa 27–6, the Pumas held the Springboks to a 16–16 draw in their home debut in Mendoza the following Saturday, a result that promised more than it delivered. Argentina had to wait two years until September 2014 for their first win in the tournament.

The Pumas were at Gold Coast in Queensland for their away match against the Wallabies in September 2012, when confronted with the news from back home that the UAR had suffered a financial fraud the union had uncovered but kept quiet.

This was an embarrassing moment for the tournament new-boys, who had brought new sponsorship to Sanzaar and some of the stolen money was part of the IRB's development fund for the Pumas.

At least two former UAR employees had been involved in falsifying signatures on cheques to pay for non-existent expenditures.

The case came to light when the UAR took the perpetrators to court in Buenos Aires on the eve of that 15 September match and Pichot, who was in Australia, had to put Sanzaar's minds at rest explaining the details.

In five Tests against leading European sides between the first and second Rugby Championships, Argentina beat Wales 26–12 in Cardiff but lost away to France and Ireland and a home series against England.

The draw with the Springboks in Mendoza in August 2012 was the best result Phelan obtained in his two Rugby Championships although he picked up bonus points in four narrow defeats, 23–19 and 25–19 by Australia in 2012 and 22–17 at home to South Africa and 14–13 away to the Wallabies in 2013.

Phelan resigned after the 2013 championship when alleged divisions in his camp were leaked, but he refused to go into detail.

'What happened isn't the best way to behave within a rugby team where there are values,' he said. 'With a repetition of these situations and having no control over them, my decision has been to step aside. My feeling is one of pain after many years of work and effort . . . I'm convinced I'm being faithful to my principles.'

Daniel Hourcade, who had been in charge of the second string Argentina XV, was quickly drafted in to take charge of the team on their November tour of Europe.

'We'd worked together, Tati and I; we had the same ideas so it was a logical replacement. There were only ten days to the tour.'

Fraud

THE PUMAS WERE becoming ever more professional going into the second decade of the millennium but the amateur UAR, failing to keep pace with their team, discovered they were being fleeced by a trusted accounts manager who had been with them for 16 years.

The UAR's senior administrators were enjoying the World Cup in New Zealand in the final months of 2011 while the accounts manager, with the help of the sales manager, were helping themselves to funds in the UAR coffers, forging signatures on cheques to pay for nonexistent expenditures.

Most of the fraudulent cheques were issued in late 2011 and early 2012, though some dated back to 2009/10, for a total of around U\$S 370,000.

'The UAR had not changed one iota in more than 100 years and was still managed like a club,' Carlos Barbieri, who was the union's treasurer at the time, told a news conference called in September 2012 to give details of the fraud when the case became public.

Since the 2007 World Cup, the UAR had grown from 35,000 to 55,000 players and it had increased its annual income from 14 million Argentine pesos to 102 million in 2012, he said.

'Yet, the finances were managed by one man who was not even a professor in economic science . . . He had the key to the safe, kept the cheque books, had the passwords to get into the accounting system and knew the passwords of his three assistants.

'What we say at the UAR is that we had lacked our Pensacola in administration.'

Pensacola in Florida is where the Pumas boosted their fitness like never before for the World Cup in France in 2007 at the state of the art Athletes' Performance facility. They returned to Pensacola before the 2011 and 2015 tournaments.

The UAR were extremely worried about how the fraud would look to their new partners in Sanzaar and the IRB who were helping to fund their high-performance centres.

The story broke while the Pumas were in Australia. It was a Friday in September 2012 and Argentina, having played South Africa twice in their first two matches in the Rugby Championship, were in Gold Coast in Queensland to face the Wallabies, having played in New Zealand the previous weekend.

Pichot, then a member of the UAR board and who was at the match, moved quickly to put Sanzaar's minds at rest.

'The fraud accelerated [the need to put] the UAR in order and fortunately the matter did not affect Argentine rugby's image abroad because we were very transparent. I stayed in Australia after the match in Gold Coast to clarify everything.'

Pichot wrote to the IRB's chief financial officer Robert Brophy telling him about the measures the UAR had since taken to bring its accounting systems into the 21st century with all payments made electronically and authorised by both its president and treasurer.

UAR president Luis Castillo also wrote to Brophy, naming the alleged principal perpetrator as former accounts manager Andrés Sánchez. The other alleged culprit is former sales manager Hernán Blanco.

'Thanks to audited processes we made to verify and test our methods of payment we were able to detect a deceitful trick made by two unfaithful employees. (Actually, I believe you know one of them, Mr Andrés Sánchez, our former accounting manager),' Castillo wrote.

'The scheme was to adulterate the treasurer's and my own signatures on pay cheques. Finally corrective actions were taken, those unfaithful people were fired and their fraud was properly denounced to the court of justice.'

The UAR said the theft came to around US$370,000, according to the rate of exchange of the Argentine peso to the dollar at the time.

Whether anyone other than the alleged culprits were involved is only going to be revealed when the case goes to court which, given the slowness of Argentina's judicial system, has, at the time of writing, yet to happen.

TWENTY-FOUR

CONTEPOMI

THE CONTEPOMI TWINS Felipe and Manuel played together for their club Newman in Buenos Aires from the juniors to the first team and at three World Cups for the Pumas including their historic third place in France in 2007.

They both also played for Bristol in the English Premiership although that was not together.

'I am so grateful for everything I experienced as a player, first for the relationship Manuel and I have with all we lived through together from when we were kids playing for our club and later when we got to the Pumas, which means playing with the best in Argentina,' says Filipe. 'And to do that with a brother, a twin, a friend, all this in one person who is Manuel . . . it's something quite unusual, that twins should play three World Cups together and have done what we did for ten years playing for the Pumas. At that level I don't know if there's been another case like it. I am very fortunate; today we can sit down and relive all those experiences – it's something spectacular.'

The closest case in Argentine rugby was the Lanza twins, Juan and Pedro, playing on the wings for the Pumas when Argentina beat France for the first time and held the All Blacks to a draw in Buenos Aires in 1985 and in two of the pool matches at the inaugural 1987 World Cup in New Zealand.

Manuel picks up the thread: 'Felipe left Newman at 22 and had a great career. He did very well at Bristol (partnering Agustín Pichot at half back) and when he was about to return to Argentina in 2003 to complete his medical studies, Leinster offered him, apart from a contract as a player, to continue studying, so that was really good for him and it was the best period of his career which I think is unique in all senses and an example to follow in terms of being able to play at the highest level and continue to study and develop other things. That led to him becoming one of the best players in history.'

Manuel did not play professional rugby until his late twenties after preferring to stay at home playing for Newman in the URBA first division championship.

'I had an offer from Bayonne but I was 19, I was at a different stage of my life and professionalism had not taken root yet. I wanted to stay and study and play for my club, so I didn't go.

'The Bristol offer came up in 2005 when I was 27, one of those surprises – it was January and I was on holiday in the Argentine summer. The 2007 World Cup was coming up and I thought it might be a good chance to go for a place in the squad at the tournament so I got my experience of leaving to play abroad at a later age. I forget if they contacted Felipe, asking about me, and he asked me if I wanted to go to Bristol. It was in mid-season and they needed a centre so I said OK and agreed – it was that simple – taking one of the two foreigner places because, like Felipe, I didn't have a [European Union] community passport.'

Manuel had one and a half seasons at Bristol and then joined Rovigo in Italy in August 2006. After the World Cup he played another season for Newman in 2008 before retiring.

Where the twins' careers differ is in great measure down to the many injuries that affected Manuel's and the few that interrupted Felipe's.

'I had eleven operations, five on my right knee alone, the first for a damaged cartilage at 19, both shoulders, a hand, my back, several injuries that, really, the timing was good because I was able to play at three World Cups. I was carrying a knee injury from the 1999 World Cup. The injuries helped me to forge a personality as a fighter, of never giving in; it's what I was dealt, the saddest and hardest part of my career. Maybe when you're young you don't do the adequate rehabilitation and try to come back too quickly and that leaves scars due to bad recovery . . . Also training was not as serious then as it is now.'

Manuel vied for the outside centre position in the 2007 team with Martin Gaitán and Gonzalo Tiesi but Gaitán suddenly suffered a heart scare after the warm-up against Wales in Cardiff three weeks before the tournament and had to give up playing, while Tiesi was carrying a knee injury. 'I was ready but only just, after a tough preparation.'

Felipe managed a fourth World Cup in New Zealand in 2011 as captain, having inherited the armband from Pichot.

'I played with many of the best Pumas and was lucky enough to have 15 years in the national team when just one is already a big deal, a gift I could not have imagined in my wildest dreams.

'Playing for your country is the highest sporting achievement and an honour but also a responsibility.'

He reeled off names he had played with like captains Pedro Sporleder and Lisandro Arbizu in teams in the late 1990s that included the likes of Federico Méndez, Roberto 'Patón' (big foot) Grau, Rolando Martin and Tati Phelan.

Then came his own generation with Pichot as leader before captaining a side with Lucas González Amorosino, Agustín Creevy and Nico Sánchez. 'I even got to play with Pablo Matera.'

Felipe was part of Alex Wyllie's squad that played the 1999 World Cup when he was 22 and not first choice but usually on the bench as a replacement fly-half.

In the quarter-final play-off in Lens, with Ireland leading 24–18 and 12 minutes to go, Wyllie sent Felipe on as fly-half and withdrew Gonzalo Quesada to full back taking Nani Corleto off.

'It was a surprise, what he did. When he sends me on as number 10 I'm asking myself why; we'd never practised with Gonza at 15.'

Five minutes later, Argentina scored the only try of the match and took the lead which they held to the end.

'It's the kind of thing that in retrospect you figure is part of New Zealanders' experience, when they work on all the options for "What if – it's being settled with kicks and I need a try so how do I do it?"

'We still hadn't taken the lead but we were celebrating because we knew Gonza would put [the conversion] over from the flag; he was our best place kicker.'

Those who played for Argentina during the Wyllie years recognise him as instrumental in the Pumas' growth and World Cup achievements from that breakthrough tournament.

'I have enormous respect and affection for him – all his players do. Wyllie was old school, a hard man, but he gave us what we needed: self-discipline in all aspects, even such apparently insignificant ones as always wearing your socks high to protect your calf muscles. He said when you're down that's the most likely place you'll get stepped on so the socks would help to protect your legs, your rivals' boots might only slide over your legs. That was something that stayed with me throughout my career. I never wore my socks low.

'He gave us a structure within which to work, starting with getting to meetings five minutes before they were due to start and Loffreda was the same so there was a seamless transition (in 2000). Tano brought this from his profession as an engineer.'

Transition

ALMOST NINE YEARS later, with many of Wyllie's players retiring after the Pumas' bronze medal success at the 2007 World Cup, came another major change in Argentina's team.

'This was a difficult transition in Argentine rugby because many players in a team who had been very successful retired suddenly and lots of young ones appeared, with the Pumas in an unexpected third place in the world. We were even third in the ranking, which was not the reality, and with me as captain and Tati [Santiago 'Tati' Phelan], who had played with me, and on top of that we had a good relationship, I'd even say friendship, as the head coach.

'Being captain was a steep learning curve with the generational change, having to learn a lot how to understand who I was leading and try to get the best out of all the players in search of what was best for the team.

'As for Tati, he was really brave because he took on something very difficult after the eight years with Tano, taking charge so young. If there's anything he was able to transmit, it was his values. They weren't, maybe, an excellent four years but he had a good World Cup and that's important.'

Argentina did what on paper looked like the best they could aspire to at the 2011 tournamen. After a narrow loss to England, they upset Scotland to finish second in their pool and reach a quarter-final against hosts New Zealand.

The Pumas lost 13–9 to England in their opening match, beat Romania 43–8, edged their decisive clash with Scotland 13–12 and beat Georgia 25–7. They lost 33–10 to the All Blacks.

What stands out for Felipe is how well the Pumas played in the tournament after being drawn in a tough group.

'I think we were very close to doing even better. What held us back a bit was not having won the first match against England. We dominated the game and should have won. England's experience got them through and the result conditioned our progress. We mustn't forget we were drawn in the group of death. There were two Tier One rivals: England and Scotland. It was the first time Scotland were eliminated in the pool stage – and by the Pumas.

'For me, what's important was how we got those results, how we played that World Cup. We played Scotland as equals and won. During that match we lost our best player, 'Corcho' (Juan Fernández Lobbe), who was injured and defended our in-goal in the final minutes in true Pumas style.

'Against New Zealand, in New Zealand, in a World Cup meant for them, we played a spectacular game in which we gave as good as we got for an hour or so and then their power and all we know about them overcame us. But that World Cup as a whole, regardless of the results, was very good in terms of our performance.'

Felipe had missed out on international rugby in 2009, still in the days when Argentina only played six Tests per season, three in June and three in November. 'I damaged my knee, the most serious injury I had, playing for Leinster against Munster in the European Cup semi-final. I had an operation in June and my plan was to do everything I could to get to November, about five months, but I missed out by a fortnight.

'I didn't have many injuries, so I was also fortunate in that, but I also trained well. In 1999 I had back surgery and then the cruciate ligament in 2009. It was another cruciate injury in 2012 but I didn't get operated because I was near the end of my career.'

Felipe wanted to experience the Rugby Championship before bowing out but missed the inaugural tournament in 2012 with back trouble.

'I told Tati I had back pains and wasn't sure I could handle the pre-season. The Pumas always have to go with the best they have; it's a priority so I told him not to count on me.'

Felipe went on tour in Europe that November and in the opening match in Wales, a 26–12 win, he damaged his posterior cruciate ligament after less than a quarter of an hour and having kicked the team's first penalty.

He ended his professional club career in 2013 and returned to Newman after a final season in France with Stade Français but said to himself, 'I'm not going to go out like this,' and worked hard on his recovery. 'I said I'll play in the June Tests (a 2–0 series loss against England and a win over Georgia) and then we'll see. I've always prioritised the Pumas out of egoism.'

He played in all six Tests of the 2013 Rugby Championship, sadly all defeats, 'not as captain because I wanted to enjoy it in another way; the leadership group in the team had changed and I had decided that was my farewell.'

He gave Newman another season in 2014 while also working with his father Carlos, an orthopaedic surgeon who won two Pumas caps in 1964, in the Centro Médico Contepomi in Buenos Aires, which they had founded together in 2009 but which only lasted a few years.

'We inaugurated it before my return and once I was back I did a university course in sports medicine, but in Argentina the medical system is different. I'm not going to make judgements but there were things I found difficult to accept.'

Felipe soon noticed a big change in Argentine domestic rugby from the game he had experienced as a young amateur 15 years previously.

'Today, it's much more competitive, from the methods clubs put into training to the time a first-team player gives to the game, it bears no comparison with what it was when I left.

'That's the big conversation we have to have [in Argentina]. Do we want to take amateur rugby to a level that is, for example, semi-professional and I don't know, but it's my question.

'Obviously, one wants to compete, find the best way to compete, but do we want an amateur game, are we being sufficiently amateur, or are we becoming too professional, even in the structure of our clubs?'

He said gone were the days when you went to watch a game played by the club's 'intermedia' team, which is essentially the reserves, and there were 30-year-olds who had previously been in the first team for ten years.

'That's no longer the case. When I returned it was all kids of 20, 21, because who's going to put in the time when you are studying or have a job?

'But if you don't put in the time you won't get picked so you say to yourself, hold on, I'll play football Tuesdays and

Thursdays with my mates and go to the club to watch the first team on Saturday.

'Today, there are lots of clubs with young squads and you've lost that thing of a player who plays for the club for 15 years, unless he's in the first team. If you've got the carrot of playing at the highest level then you do it.

'But most quit at 24, 25 because it's a heavy toll as an amateur having to train Monday, Tuesday and Thursday and find time to go to the gym three times a week and play a match on Saturdays – it's almost like a pro.'

This reflects a change at national team level as more young players take up rugby seriously. Senior squads at many clubs have enough players for reserve and third teams as well as an under-23 side.

Coaching

IN 2015, PUMAS head coach Daniel Hourcade asked Felipe if he would like to take charge of Argentina XV, the country's second-string team, who were going to take part in the Nations Cup in Romania.

Coaching appealed to him and in 2016 he was offered a post on the staff of the Jaguares, the new Super Rugby franchise, Argentina's first professional team, under head coach Raúl Pérez.

'I started getting more involved in the UAR, the professional era was starting and the whole professional system in Argentina was very good up to the age of 20 but there was no place for the under-23s which is [equivalent to] the academies here [in Europe].

'So in 2017 I proposed that Argentina XV should be converted into a development team, which wasn't easy because it was a kind of pseudo professionalism with difficulties posed by the amateur clubs in terms of availability. I learnt that there are times when you have to be more selfish and not try to please everyone.

'It was a good experience but I realised that if I wanted to progress in my career I would have to go abroad and that's when the Leinster option [to become the province's backs coach] came up three years ago. I have since renewed for another two years.'

Felipe noted there were several former Pumas, all of whom he played alongside at some stage, making a name for themselves as coaches.

Gonzalo Quesada, who steered the Jaguares to the Super Rugby final in his first season in charge, returned to Stade Français when the franchise was disbanded after the southern hemisphere competition was fragmented as a result of the coronavirus pandemic.

Juan 'Corcho' Fernández Lobbe was assistant to Mario Ledesma with the Pumas from the start of the 2023 World Cup cycle while his elder brother Nacho took charge of Argentina XV.

'It's a generational thing and what we all have is that experience as players, but being a coach is a lot more than just the game and that's the challenge of developing and learning. There are courses. I've got a leadership and management diploma and you go feeding on other aspects that aren't so obvious because you experienced other things as a player. You don't need to tell me what it's like to play at Twickenham, I played there, but I do have to learn to teach because a coach is like a master.'

Felipe became the third Argentine to be inducted into World Rugby's Hall of Fame in 2017 after Hugo Porta (2008) and Agustín Pichot (2011).

TWENTY-FIVE

ATTACK!

'YOU'D SEE SIX players coming at you down the same channel and you didn't know what was going to happen; they had so many options – I liked that, a lot of strategy. Eddie Jones's (Australia) side were so good, remember them? How well they played.

'They were my model, not copy and paste, but that idea of an unpredictable team with variety, daring, taking risks to the limit. I think it's the only way to achieve great things, to beat the [rugby] powers.'

Daniel 'Huevo' Hourcade speaks enthusiastically about his rugby ideal and the high points of his tenure as head coach of the Pumas.

His time with the Pumas can be illustrated with a steep graph like a silhouette of the peaks in the Andes range not far west of his native Tucumán.

A great admirer of Australian rugby, the Pumas side Hourcade steered to the World Cup semi-finals in England in 2015 left you breathless, like being up one of those Andean mountains.

An exciting climb including Rugby Championship victories over Australia in 2014 and South Africa in 2015 reached a summit with Argentina's quarter-final victory over Ireland in Cardiff.

However, in terms of results, it was mostly back down the mountain from 2016 despite another win over the Springboks in Salta. It had a lot to do with playing against three of the world's top half dozen teams twice every year and always as underdogs.

Eddie Jones's England also gave him a prolonged headache with four defeats in 12 months. These included surrendering the lead in the dying minutes of a first Test defeat by 38–34 in a home series the Pumas lost 2–0 in June 2017 against an England squad with many debutants while most of the first team were on tour with the Lions.

This had a detrimental effect on the Pumas' ranking when it came to the draw for the 2019 World Cup in Japan. In Hourcade's four years in charge, wins against France twice, Italy four times, Georgia and Japan marginally improved a record of only three victories in 21 Rugby Championship matches.

Hourcade says he and his coaching staff could see improvements from Test to Test in the style of play they were seeking. But nearly always losing gradually undermined his work.

When he announced he was resigning in June 2018 after a home series defeat by Wales, he had the feeling a wedge had appeared between him and his players.

Portugal

DANIEL HOURCADE, NICKNAMED Huevo by his brother who thought his head looked like an egg when they were kids, played at scrum-half for Universitario RC of Tucumán, retiring in 1992.

He took his early coaching steps with his club before taking on UAR roles including Argentina's Sevens team.

During his travels in charge of the Sevens team on the world circuit in the early 2000s, Hourcade was offered a club job in Portugal.

Unsure about such a big decision to leave an organised life in Argentina in his forties, he went on a three-month reconnaissance.

'I went for three months and stayed for about six years.

'In those days, 2004, there was no chance of thinking about dedicating your time professionally to rugby, at least in Argentina and even less as a coach.'

Coaching Grupo Desportivo Direito with an impressive counter-attacking game led to him being asked to assist the Portugal head coach on the country's marathon, 18–match qualifying campaign to reach the 2007 World Cup.

He was visited in Lisbon by Agustín Pichot and Juan Martín Hernández, who were then playing at Stade Français in Paris, for a home match against Russia.

'They were two stars, and you can imagine what it was like to have them at the hotel; the team took great motivation from it.

'The Portuguese players are small but very courageous. They defended and counter-attacked well against the giants of Georgia, Russia and Romania, and when they had the ball they made a difference.'

Hourcade would visit Paris occasionally at a time when Stade Français had a large group of Argentines – also including Nani Corleto, Lucas Borges and Rodrigo Roncero – he had trained in different national teams back home. 'Fabien Galthié was their coach; I'd stay a week, watch and learn.

'The 2007 World Cup in France, which has more than 3 million Portuguese immigrants, was a landmark moment for Portugal's rugby. They were the weakest team in the tournament but they filled the stadiums.'

After the World Cup, Hourcade coached Rouen in France's Federal 1 championship, the rung below the fully professional Top 14 and D2 divisions, turning down an offer from Pichot to work in the high-performance programme in Argentina because it meant not coaching a team.

He returned to Portugal in 2009 tempted by a project for a professional Iberian league but within two months he was offered a job back home that did appeal, to take charge of the Pampas XV.

Pampas

THE PAMPAS WERE a key component of Argentina's plan to build up a pool of players who would go on to become professionals without having to join clubs abroad, and feed the Pumas – and eventually a franchise.

'If I'd stayed in Portugal I would have done so gladly but they didn't put any constraints on me. "How are we going to deny you the chance with a national team of your country?"

'They behaved brilliantly towards me and I'm eternally grateful to them because that project was up to a point based on my involvement after what the World Cup had meant to them.'

The Pampas played in South Africa's Vodacom Cup, a level below the Currie Cup, from 2010 to 2013 with Hourcade coaching them unbeaten to the title in 2011. They also won the Pacific Rugby Cup unbeaten in 2014 and in 2015 before being disbanded when Argentina entered the Jaguares franchise, made up largely of former Pampas players, in Super Rugby in 2016.

What stood out from the Pampas squad for Hourcade was their togetherness while based for three months in virtual isolation in the quiet city of Potchefstroom in South Africa's North West Province.

'Our South African base in Potchefstroom had spectacular training facilities, but we spent three months in the place with nothing to do, nowhere to go out because it was dangerous. We had everything but it was isolated. And there was only three hours a day of team activity.

'Living together is not easy, with so much spare time, without being able to go out for a coffee. We'd go once a week to a shopping mall 50 kilometres away by coach, all together – that was our outing.

'The day we came home we all cried because we didn't want it to end; we'd formed not just a group but a whole family.'

Nine players from Hourcade's Vodacom Cup-winning side were included by Tati Phelan in his Pumas squad at the 2011 World Cup in New Zealand.

'In 2003 and 2007, the World Cup squad was players who played in Europe. In 2011, nine Pampas went to the World Cup, reared in Argentina, and another four were reserves.

'The objective of the training centres was beginning to bear fruit, moulding our players in our country without them having to go abroad to improve their game which is what had happened after 1999.

'But after 2007, many retired and there was no project to back up all that effort those kids had made. Agustín, who was one of them, took off his rugby shirt and put on a suit and started to fight so Argentina could have a plan to be able to compete at the highest level with a regular competition.'

Hourcade was asked to take the Pumas on their European tour in November 2013 after Phelan's resignation and the following season was offered a contract taking in the next two World Cups until 2019 – though to be revised approximately every two years.

He became the third Argentine-born head coach who had not played for the Pumas after Michingo O'Reilly in the 1980s and Alejandro Petra in 1995 and only the second, after Petra, who was not from Buenos Aires.

Hourcade could have retained veteran back-row forward Juan Martín Fernández Lobbe as captain but opted for hooker Agustín Creevy, who had led his Pampas side.

'I knew his qualities as a group leader and believed that was what was needed at the time.' Creevy was between two generations of players and made the perfect nexus.

England 2015

THERE WERE 15 months to go to the World Cup when Hourcade made his proper start as head coach in the June Test window in 2014, a home series lost 2–0 against Six Nations champions Ireland, 29–17 and 23–17, followed by a 21–19 defeat by Scotland.

In terms of matches, there were just 12 Tests to try out new players, the young ones who had come through Pampas XV and the second string Argentina XV.

He also had to win over the veterans of the 2007 and 2011 World Cups and bear out what Graham Henry had told Phelan's Pumas – that they needed to score more tries.

'We had to attack more, take more risks, get the players who had been abroad for some time to know and trust those being trained in our country.

'We saw [the team's] evolution at the World Cup when we played against teams like Georgia and beat them by a large margin. They are not an easy team, for us or anyone. Tonga too, remember they beat France (in 2011).

'We scored the most points in the group phase, something that was unusual with Argentina, and although we lost our first match against New Zealand it wasn't by much and we were dominating until the 60th minute.

'Argentina had often played well against the All Blacks but never dominated them. But they are what they are and turned it round with the replacements.

'They were a machine but we were happy, not with the result of course, but we managed what we had never done before in terms of the objectives we had and that showed we had progressed a lot.

'We had beaten South Africa in the Rugby Championship and played a very good match against the All Blacks and won the rest of our pool and reached the quarter-finals to face Ireland, who were among the favourites to reach the final, and beat them clearly.

'We were content because we could see and measure our evolution.'

Like Gonzalo Quesada in 1999, fly-half Nicolás Sánchez was the top scorer at the World Cup with 97 points and the Pumas had excited the crowds with their rugby but they had lost three matches against their southern hemisphere rivals: New Zealand in the pool, Australia in their semi-final and South Africa in the third place play-off.

Jaguares

THE NEXT STAGE in Argentina's development was entering a franchise, with 40 professional players, in Super Rugby in 2016.

'We needed to broaden our player base because it was very small but we didn't have tournaments to play, and when we started to compete with a professional team, Jaguares in 2016, it was just that, one team,' said Hourcade.

Argentina may have had an advantage in being together all season, as Jaguares and then Pumas, but their opponents had five or six franchises from which to pick their internationals with more internal competition for places.

'If there is something that distinguishes an Argentine player it's his commitment, but internal competition is fundamental as is the frequency of matches.'

With two franchises, hookers Creevy and Julián Montoya, his Jaguares reserve, would have both played regularly, as would scrum-halves Martín Landajo and Tomás Cubelli, instead of one starting and the other finishing a match.

'Having only one team [to draw from] limits you in quantity, internal competition and minutes. We had 40 players that needed to play. The only advantage was being a team who were together all year but the exhaustion was terrible.'

In two decades, Argentina's professionals went from playing six matches a year in the two Test windows to 12 when they entered the Rugby Championship in 2012 and 28 including 16 Super Rugby fixtures from 2016.

Fly-half Santiago 'Rete' González Iglesias, who usually started on the bench during his Pumas career, put it succinctly when he said: 'Today, the players who are replacements for the Pumas come from being replacements with Jaguares.

'The replacements in the British Test teams are first-choice stars in their club sides, likewise the New Zealanders because they have several franchises [to pick from] and nowadays replacements are very important; they end up settling a match.'

Hourcade added: 'Our third hooker, Facundo Bosch, played 130 minutes all year. Due to lack of game time he went off to France even though [at the time] the European exiles were banned from playing for the Pumas. But what can you say to that kid?'

The UAR had decided they would select Pumas squads entirely from home-based players once the Jaguares franchise was up and running.

'And on top of everything, there was the political problem (from 2016) that the Buenos Aires players were banned by their union URBA from playing for their [amateur] clubs, so when they weren't in a Super Rugby match squad they didn't play at all.' This rule was in the URBA statutes whereas the other provincial unions allowed their players to play club rugby whenever available.

'If we'd had two teams it would have been different. Three would be ideal but impossible to even consider economically.

'We had been fighting for more competition so we're not now going to go complaining. No, that was our reality and we had to adapt though it was far from ideal.'

Hourcade's Pumas played in four Rugby Championships, with a 21–17 win against Australia and three bonus points in 2014 and one win and one bonus point in 2015 when, being a World Cup year, it was a shorter, three-match tournament and their 37–25 victory over South Africa in Durban meant they avoided the wooden spoon for the first time.

In 2016, the Pumas beat the Springboks 26–24 at home but finished bottom of the table again while 2017 was Argentina's worst season with zero points.

After the World Cup, victories were scarce – against France in a shared home series, South Africa, Japan, Georgia and Italy – and in June 2018 Hourcade resigned after losing a home series to Wales 2–0 and before a meeting with Scotland the following weekend in the northern city of Resistencia.

There was not much resistance there as his Pumas were crushed 44–15, a record win for Scotland in Argentina, with British match reports calling their out-of-character performance woeful and limp.

Hourcade appeared to have lost support among his players while a different coaching regime headed by Mario Ledesma, in charge of virtually the same squad in the Jaguares franchise, had the two teams pulling in different directions. The two men did not share the same rugby philosophy.

TWENTY-SIX

'EL MAGO'

EL MAGO KICKED sublime drop goals with either foot, curled brilliant touch finders deep into opposition territory with either side of his instep, gave accurate passes from layoffs or palming the ball on from one player to the next in the line or throwing it half the width of the field to a man on the wing.

The skills that Juan Martín Hernández displayed on the rugby field looked effortless but, as with all top sports personalities, everything he did so well came from the hard work he put in to hone his talents.

'Everything he did came off, but not by chance, rather because he worked incredibly hard on the details; he was a perfectionist,' says Tano Loffreda.

'He's the most talented player I had the privilege to coach, a kid who made the complicated things look easy, who took risks, managed time and space perfectly, had peripheral vision, a foot like a glove and a devastating tackle,' purrs Huevo Hourcade.

'You have an advantage with a player like Hernández, gifted as a sportsman and our good fortune to have been born Argentine,' adds prop Rodrigo Roncero, his teammate at Deportiva Francesa, their first club in Buenos Aires, Stade Français and in the Pumas.

Juan Martín Hernández helped Argentina reach the semi-finals in two World Cups, as fly-half in France in 2007 under Loffreda when he was 25 and eight years later in England at inside centre for Hourcade.

Injuries, at times the result of his bravery and commitment to defence, prevented him from playing in the 2011 World Cup in New Zealand in his prime, denying him many more caps than the 74 he retired with.

He went three years without a Test match from a win over England in Salta in June 2009 to his comeback for Argentina's Rugby Championship debut against South Africa in Cape Town in August 2012.

During that period he joined the Sharks in Durban from Stade Français with the aim of playing in Super Rugby but a back injury limited him to nine matches in the Currie Cup that season.

He finally got his Super Rugby wish when he signed up for the Jaguares franchise, which joined Super Rugby in 2016, after another five years in France with Racing Metro and Toulon.

Having begun his professional career with Stade Français at full back and played his early Test matches there, 'Le Magicien' as he was known by his Parisian admirers played at fly-half, his favourite position, when Argentina won the bronze medal at the 2007 World Cup.

Hernández remained Argentina's first choice fly-half for seven years – apart from the injury absences – before taking a key midfield role for Hourcade from the 2014 Rugby Championship.

'My game plan was always with two playmakers and Juani in midfield helped Nico Sánchez a lot, above all with decision-making, and so that we had two possibilities to generate the dynamic and expansive game we sought.

'Although he had played in different positions, his favourite was at 10 so I spoke to him to tell him my game plan and what I hoped for from him.

'He told me he would never argue with the coach's decisions to which I replied that I knew he might say that but that I needed to be sure whether he really felt comfortable in that inside centre position, so we agreed we would try it in some matches and then talk again.

'After two or three Tests in the 2014 Rugby Championship he told me he felt really good and enjoyed playing there.

'He always put the team first and was key in that position and when he had the chance to play at 10, which he really loved, it was in many ways a similar job to what he did at 12.'

That chance came up in Durban in August 2015 when Hourcade picked Hernández at fly-half in 11 changes from the previous Test, a crushing 34–9 defeat against Australia in Mendoza – the venue where they had beaten the Wallabies 21–17 the previous year – and he inspired Argentina to their first victory over South Africa and the first time the Pumas avoided the Rugby Championship's wooden spoon.

Hernández had missed the Australia defeat and an opening 39–18 loss to New Zealand in Christchurch in a shorter, three-Test tournament in a World Cup year and the following month he was back at 12 playing outside Sánchez in England as part of Argentina's run to the semi-finals.

Highs and lows

EL MAGO'S PUMAS career was marked by the wonderful atmosphere that pervaded the team that won the 2007 World Cup bronze medal, the long and difficult recovery from a serious back operation two years later, missing the 2011 tournament after a knee injury and the tears of joy at having overcome those hardships with another place in the semi-finals in 2015.

'The loveliest moment of my career was the 2007 World Cup without a doubt, what that group of players achieved, how hard and well they worked and where they had come from.

'That group, the leaders, emerged at the 1999 World Cup which I watched on TV and they were my idols, qualifying for the quarter-finals for the first time and sparking a Pumamanía.

'I saw them defend against Ireland and said to myself, "One day I want to be one of those players," – how they threw themselves down to defend their in-goal, it looked spectacular.

'Four years later, I was part of the squad at the 2003 World Cup, again facing Ireland and this time it was Argentina's turn to lose, by one point almost at the end of the match, and those players who were young in 1999 were beginning to have leading roles.

'By then there were several Argentine players in European rugby and expectations were high for the Pumas to qualify and repeat or even improve on the previous World Cup.

'The team failed to get past the first round and that hurt, but that forged something internal and motivated their preparation for 2007, because the build-up to 2003 was perhaps not the best with players split between the many who were in Europe and a similar number in Argentina.

'We tried to all be on the same wavelength but couldn't because of the lack of a structure for training and being together.

'So the team took strength from overcoming those weaknesses, building on the players who had been part of the success in 1999 and the frustration in 2003. That produced a spectacular preparation for 2007.

'What stands out for me in 2007 is the whole group of players, what they had been through to then achieve something big – third place and a bronze medal is just window dressing, but the passion of that group on and off the field.'

After six seasons at Stade Français, including two French top-flight titles and finishing runners-up in the Heineken Cup in 2005, Hernández chose to test himself in Super Rugby.

'We had won two leagues and came very close in the European Cup, losing the final to Toulouse. They levelled the score near the end and we went to extra time, they scored a penalty and a drop and we ran out of gas.

'I had done well in European rugby and wanted to go to the best rugby in the world, which I believed was Super Rugby, which was called Super 14 at the time. I wanted to face the best.'

He could have gone to Auckland but opted for the Sharks on a one-year contract from July 2009, having visited and liked Durban with the Pumitas when he was 19.

'South Africa had a great team at the time. The Springboks were made up mainly of the Sharks forwards and the Bulls backs and I told myself I would be playing with that pack and Ruan Pienaar, Rory Kockott or Charl McLeod, no matter which of the three, a pack that goes forwards with a scrum-half who passes well, playing fly-half there in the South African style of pressure, kicking and tackling, I thought that game fitted me well.

'I had a wonderful time but I couldn't live it to the full. We lost the Currie Cup semi-final to the Cheetahs and I had a lot of pain in my back due to a bone deformity from birth which appeared in South Africa. Many people thought it was an injury caused by the intensity of the game in South Africa but that's not so; I had suffered pains long before.'

Hernández was faced with a critical choice: having a corrective operation that would allow him to get back in time for the Super 14 or following the recommendation of his and the Pumas' orthopaedic specialist Mario Larrain in Argentina to deal with the root cause, a year and a half before the World Cup in New Zealand.

'When I told the South Africans I was going to have the bigger operation with a longer recovery period they said, "You're crazy; you might never play rugby again and maybe not any other sport." But I came to Argentina to be operated on by surgeon Jorge Salvat (father of the 1995 Pumas captain Sebastián Salvat) who said, "Juan, I'm going to operate on you, you'll play again and you'll be fine," and it was a good decision.'

Before the operation, Hernández returned to Paris to sign a contract with Racing Metro for the next French season. 'They took a chance on me, knowing the risks of such an investment.'

It took ten tough months of rehabilitation to get back to playing but after half a dozen matches, when he was feeling fully confident and strong, he suffered a knee injury in an away match against Bourgoin, damaging his right cruciate ligament as he went down under the weight of a high tackle by a big opponent six months before the 2011 World Cup.

'I tried an immediate recovery with an operation in Argentina but it was crazy. I got to the date when the Pumas squad list was announced without any matches. You don't go to a World Cup to try out your knee but rather having earned your place on the field and I didn't get that chance.

'It was a huge disappointment because I did everything I could to get there, above all after taking that risky decision to fix my back, and it was something else that restricted me.

'It wasn't so much missing out on being with the team that was being built and I would have liked to have been a part of that, but because of how much I fought and what a bad time I had after two hard rehabilitations, particularly with my back, in a rigid corset for four months, hardly moving in bed, only taking it off to bathe, and my first son had been born and I couldn't pick him up and hold him in my arms. I had lost 15 kilos and was plagued by doubts about whether I would be able to play rugby again and how I would carry on building my family. I took hard decisions that I was unable to see through by not going to the World Cup.

'But I was able to play again and get payback in 2015. After a back operation and two on my knee, a bit older, helping the team from another position, not standing out so much in my individual actions, I returned to the highest level.

'Like with everything, sometimes you agree with the coach and sometimes not, but the team comes first and the position they wanted me in and the job they wanted from me at inside centre is where I did my bit for the team during the Hourcade period.

'Clearly, the 2015 World Cup was another peak in my career. The quarter-final against Ireland at the Millennium Stadium is surely one of the matches I will remember most in my life, along with a few others, because of what came before, missing the previous World Cup. After a lot of physical, mental and family effort, I got my new chance of another semi-final and the dream of playing in a final and winning the World Cup.

'So when we beat Ireland, when you do a lap of honour waving to the whole stadium, the fans, I felt very emotional and because I was on my own at that moment I started feeling some tears for what I'd overcome, the resilience, that there is always revenge, and we'd built a really good team, so it hit me and I wept. I keep that image in my mind.

'On top of that, the match was spectacular, scoring nice tries, Juan Fernández Lobbe having a great match and the whole team defending Pumas-style.

'It was one of the peaks. I mentioned 2007 as a group of players, 2015 is also very much in my mind in that moment of solitude, like a caress and a prize to myself for the way I fought to be there again.'

Joining the Jaguares after a season at Toulon, Hernández finally got his chance to play Super Rugby.

'With the Jaguares, it was building a new group, looking for a new identity, passing team values on to younger players – that was my main contribution more than on the field, as one of the veterans along with Juan Manuel Leguizamón.

'In Super Rugby there isn't the same pressure to win as in Test rugby; the game is more open. In a Test match you do everything possible to win so you don't take as many risks; there's more attention to the details. All the preparation time you have in a club, you don't get in a national team, so you have to play to your strengths.'

Hernández did not close out his career playing again for his first club, Deportiva Francesa, like some of his Pumas teammates had done on returning home, getting back into the amateur game.

'In my last match for Jaguares, against the Reds, I suffered a partial rupture of my cruciate in the knee I had already had surgery on twice for the same thing and I didn't want a third operation – the knee rehab at 35 is not the same as when you're younger – so I decided to retire from rugby.

'Rugby gave me a lot and I gave it what I could. I preferred to dedicate myself to a sport suitable for my kids which is kicking a ball about in the garden of my home or at the club. I'm not a coach, I just help out now and again at the club; my brother coaches a junior division team and I help him out a bit with the three-quarters.'

It all began with sound advice from his father the day he was called up for the first time to the Pumas.

'Being a Puma is what my father told me the day I was picked for the first time: it's a matter of pride, first, and it's also a responsibility towards the kids, like when I was young and I watched my idols, the heroes of that time wearing the Pumas colours and we, at the club, would mimic some of Agustín's runs or Arbizu's changes of pace and admire Tati Phelan's commitment. So now that I occupied that place because I'd been chosen, I had to transmit the Pumas' values to younger kids.'

Reflecting on Agustín Pichot's belief that he had a 'camaraderie of the game' with Felipe Contepomi and Hernández, El Mago called it 'a connection through a love of sport.

'We had an identical view of sport. Today rugby is very structured and there are lots of systems, for defence, for attack, for a kicking game. We felt free on the rugby pitch to have fun doing what we wanted to. In reality we set out to disconcert our opponents, to express ourselves freely and have fun.'

TWENTY-SEVEN

SANZAAR

AFTER ALEX WYLLIE as a coach in the 1990s and Graham Henry as a technical advisor to the Pumas in the early Rugby Championship period, another New Zealander, Greg Peters, became general manager of the Argentine union to lead the country's entry to Super Rugby.

'By 2012 we had the Pumas in the Rugby Championship and were working towards having Argentina in Super Rugby,' Peters said of his time in his previous job as chief executive officer of the four-nation southern hemisphere Sanzaar group in Sydney from 2010.

'Argentina realised that to be successful long term they had to have their players back from Europe and not just flying in and out to play for the Pumas. That was the thrust of getting them into Super Rugby and also becoming a full-blown member of Sanzaar with a double A in the middle, which happened for the period of 2016 to 2020.

'I got friendly with Agustín Pichot towards the end of my time with Sanzaar and I'd done what I could there and we were just renegotiating the broadcasting deal so it was kind of time to look for a new horizon and Agustín suggested to me, "Why don't you come to Argentina and do this?"

'This was part of Pichot's Mr Rugby role with Argentina, not as a jacket-and-tie member of the UAR board but the man making all the big decisions.'

Peters lived in Argentina for around 18 months helping the Jaguares – the franchise that came to provide the Pumas with almost all their players – settle into Super Rugby as the country's only professional team in the 2016 season.

'Argentina had the massive power of Agustín Pichot, a charismatic leader, and until his unfortunate demise at World Rugby he was carrying Sanzaar.

'But he's still in the background. Nothing would happen without him knowing, it's just the way Argentina works, big personalities and he is massive but not in a formal sense. When I was there he didn't actually hold a formal role within the union, he was this person who was able to make things happen and everyone listened to him.'

Peters said Pichot's standing is also why the UAR fraud case had no big repercussions within Sanzaar or World Rugby.

'No one has the gravitas he had or has, particularly in Sanzaar. All of the Sanzaar unions were behind him to lead change so he provided this massive amount of credibility to the UAR and Argentina.

'He got the Pumas to where they were. It was his leadership from 2007 onwards that said we've got to put in a high-performance plan, we've got to get the union modernised, we've got to get into the Rugby Championship, we've got to get into Sanzaar – he drove all that.'

Peters helped the UAR overcome many obstacles as they set up the Jaguares, which involved players returning home to sign contracts with the UAR that tied them to the Jaguares and, by extension, guaranteed they were eligible for the Pumas.

'The whole system of contracting players on a multi-year basis, the commercialisation of the Jaguares and working with the Sanzaar way of doing things, given [Argentina's geographical] isolation, really was a big challenge because every away game was not just the Blues going down the road to play the Chiefs.

'We were ten hours minimum from South Africa which was our closest away game. And once Air New Zealand started the route [from Buenos Aires] to Auckland, which has gone now unfortunately, it was quicker to get to Auckland on a 14-hour flight than it was to get to Johannesburg. So our closest away game was probably the Blues.

'We were facing a myriad of challenges because, for example, just to get the Nike kit into Argentina was a massive challenge. Nike had a factory in Argentina but it couldn't make the kit we needed so we had to import that, which at the time was a very challenging process because of import restrictions. Even our GPX got held up in customs for months; we had a lot of challenges which other unions or teams in Super Rugby didn't face.

'That's one of the strengths of the people in Argentina, the rugby people – you didn't hear one word of complaint about anything. Yet when I was CEO of the Hurricanes if I had put that team through some of the things the Jaguares and Pumas had to go through we would have had a revolt, so it's just a wonderful way they approached it – nothing was too much of a problem, just get on with it, don't let it faze you. It was a really special time and taught me a lot about how people approach adversity.

'The uniqueness of Argentine rugby is the strength of the amateur game, the special place it has in the clubs as part of the fabric of rugby and which we'd lost in Australia and New Zealand and potentially the UK – the amateur club heart and soul of the game.'

Peters returned home to New Zealand in 2018 but kept a keen interest in Argentine rugby, watching the Jaguares breach the pool phase of Super Rugby in their third season in 2018 and reach the final in 2019.

That, however, was how long the Jaguares adventure lasted. The team was disbanded in 2020 owing to the coronavirus pandemic that disrupted Super Rugby in its most recent international format. New Zealand and Australia created their own domestic tournaments. South African teams joined what was previously known as the Celtic League, which became the PRO14 and from 2021 the United Rugby Championship. This included teams from Ireland, Scotland, Wales and Italy, with the convenience of the same time zone.

'It's really sad [after] the amount of work and the willingness of people to come back from Europe and base themselves in Buenos Aires again and the spirit that got the Jaguares to the final in 2019.

'And obviously they were going to be a force with a big part of the squad being the Pumas themselves, if they could handle the adversity of the travel and the week in, week out grind of Super Rugby where there's just nowhere to hide; you can't have a bad day in Super Rugby of that era.

'I can't see it coming back to the way it was and including Argentina, which is sad, but it's also a good opportunity for Argentina and other unions in South America to focus on the Americas which was always the long game but it's been brought forward a bit.

'Super Liga Americana de Rugby (SLAR) is an exciting development and how you link in with the US and Canada; the Americas Rugby Championship, which we also started in 2016, was a fantastic development.

'They can start building that area and in my view ultimately it was always going to be the long game; some linkage with South Africa but also growing the Americas which is where the opportunity is.

'Maybe it's five years ahead of where it could have been in the natural development of that and the potential of Uruguay, Chile and Brazil to grow is massive. Having to revert to that rather than continue to play in Super Rugby is about five years ahead of time.'

The Americas Rugby Championship is a modern expansion from the South American Championship which began in 1951 and Argentina always won unbeaten, except in 1981 when they did not take part, and which they took part in until 2013.

Since then Argentina have taken part in regional competitions with their second string team, Argentina XV. The six-nation tournament which began in 2016 includes Argentina XV plus the Test sides from Brazil, Canada, Chile, United States and Uruguay. Argentina XV and United States have two titles each. The tournament was cancelled in 2020 because of Covid.

Meanwhile, the SLAR was played in 2021 with six franchises from six South American countries including Argentina's Jaguares XV, many of whom would have been in the Super Rugby Jaguares side had that competition continued. All six franchises had Argentine coaches with several Argentine players in the other five sides.

TWENTY-EIGHT

LEDESMA

ARGENTINA WENT BACK to basics under Mario Ledesma: forward play needed a revamp but time was short to prepare for a tough pool at the World Cup in Japan 13 months away.

Ledesma had spent 16 years living abroad as a player, helping Clermont reach four consecutive French Top 14 finals and finally winning the title at the fourth attempt in 2010, and later as a coach.

Having spent two years with Michael Cheika as the Wallabies' forwards coach in Australia, he returned home to Argentina in 2017 to take over from Raúl 'Aspirina' Pérez as coach of Jaguares in their third season in Super Rugby in 2018.

He steered the Jaguares to a place in the last eight for the first time after finishing second behind the Lions in the South African Conference.

The Jaguares beat the Lions 49–35 in Buenos Aires and lost 47–27 to them away in the pool stage. Then they lost their quarter-final 40–23 to the same opponents in Johannesburg.

Ledesma did not get a second chance with the Jaguares although he would be working with the same players as the new head coach of the Pumas from August 2018, replacing Hourcade.

The Pumas managed two wins for the first time in the Rugby Championship that year, 32–19 at home to the Springboks and 23–19 away to Australia, but still finished bottom of the standings despite their best points tally of eight.

What had looked like a good end to a fine tournament for the Pumas midway through their final match at home to Australia in Mendoza ended in huge disappointment – and a return to previous woes of failing to close out matches in the final quarter when they were ahead.

Argentina led 31–7 at half-time after scoring four tries to one but the Wallabies, after a half-time roasting from Cheika, turned the game on its head in the second half taking their tally to five tries and winning 45–34.

Santiago González Iglesias, who had replaced the injured Nicolás Sánchez at fly-half on the half hour, scored the fourth try a minute after coming on, converted it and kicked a penalty before the interval. He added a second penalty for Argentina's only points of the second half.

Former Pumas fly-half Gonzalo Quesada, Ledesma's teammate at two World Cups who had made a name for himself as a coach in France, particularly at Stade Français, took over the Jaguares for the 2019 Super Rugby season. Quesada steered the team to first place in the South African Conference and to the final where they lost 19–3 to Crusaders in Christchurch. He was surprisingly not added to the Pumas World Cup staff.

Ledesma had not expected the Jaguares to go so far, counting on the players getting a break and returning to training as Pumas one or two weeks sooner than they did, although their form had seemed to augur well for the Rugby Championship and World Cup in Japan.

Believing Argentina had a good chance to beat New Zealand for the first time, Ledesma chose to pick the same players who were runners-up in the Super Rugby tournament to face the All Blacks in their opening Rugby Championship match in Buenos Aires two weeks later.

It turned out to be a match too far for the players and they were unable to recover from going 20–9 behind in a first half marked by lock Brodie Retallick's interception try after running from New Zealand's 22.

Emiliano Boffelli scored a fine try early in the second half from a high cross-field kick to the far corner by Sánchez but the Pumas lost 20–16 after failing to capitalise on their throw at a lineout five metres out in the final action of the match.

Critics said the decision not to rest some first choice Jaguares for the All Blacks match had a knock-on effect in the rest of the three-match tournament, in which the Pumas finished bottom, and the World Cup.

Argentina had lost nine Tests in a row going into the World Cup in Japan, twice against each of their three southern hemisphere rivals plus Ireland, Scotland and France on tour in November 2018.

Ledesma put all his cards on beating France in Argentina's opening match, the key in a pool that also included title favourites England.

The Pumas had a poor first half and the French dominated with tries by Gaël Fickou and Antoine Dupont to lead 20–3 at half-time.

But they still might have achieved what would have been the greatest second-half comeback in a World Cup, surpassing their own record victory over Samoa in 1999 when they had been 16–3 down at the interval and had won 32–16.

The Pumas clawed their way back to lead 21–20 with a penalty from replacement fly-half Benjamín Urdapilleta with ten minutes to go following tries from forwards Guido Petti and Julián Montoya.

But replacement fly-half Camille Lopez restored France's lead with a drop goal and Boffelli's huge place kick from inside Argentina's half drifted narrowly wide in the dying minutes, leaving France 23–21 winners.

Argentina beat Tonga 28–12 before meeting England in a

match they had to win to retain any hopes of reaching the knockout stage, a task that became virtually impossible with an early red card for lock Tomás Lavanini for a dangerous shoulder charge on Owen Farrell.

A man short for more than an hour, the Pumas went down 39–10 to their fifth consecutive defeat by Eddie Jones's England, who scored six tries.

Argentina bowed out with a 47–17 win over the United States, while England and France progressed.

Scrum DNA

LEDESMA HIGHLIGHTED A handicap when he took charge of the Pumas, something he had no doubt become aware of coaching the Jaguares but which did not matter quite as much given the more open kind of game played in that competition with less emphasis on scrummaging and strategic kicking.

Argentina had lost their renowned power in the scrum, their DNA as he called it, as a result of a rule introduced in the country's domestic competitions after injuries left several forwards paralysed.

The UAR ruled in 2016 that scrums would be penalised for pushing more than one and a half metres after the late San Isidro Club prop Jerónimo Bello was left disabled from a collapsed scrum in a Buenos Aires first division match in September 2016, the fourth serious injury in a year. Only five-metre scrums were exempt.

'Not only does it weaken Argentine scrummaging culture, which is part of our DNA, but it's also part of a forward's soul,' Ledesma said during Argentina's tour of Europe in November 2018 when they lost to Ireland, France and Scotland.

'Today, scrums in Argentina last five or six seconds which is why the kids who come to us from their clubs are surprised by the hardness of a scrum and if it lasts more than ten seconds it discomforts them in a manner of speaking.

'You have to be able to enjoy that kind of wrestling and [understand] the bearing it has on other areas of the game. The cohesion you achieve in a team with a solid scrum and the psychological boost [you get] from that is immeasurable.'

The ban on a free shove – part of a nationwide programme called Rugby Seguro (safe rugby) aimed at protecting players from serious injury – was lifted in 2019 but work has continued to eliminate dangers in the scrum due to poor and illicit practices.

'The best thing we achieved is that now everyone knows you have to look after yourself and your rival,' said Rugby Seguro president Néstor Galán. 'We needed a cultural change, addressing fairness and honesty in scrummaging and in the game itself.'

Ledesma named Eduardo Fernández Gill, an experienced former national junior teams coach who specialised in scrummaging, to lead a nationwide search for forward talent.

'Maori'

AGUSTÍN CREEVY WAS no newcomer to Steve Hansen when Argentina played their first Rugby Championship in 2012, which was also the New Zealander's first as All Blacks head coach.

Seven years earlier in Mendoza, Hansen toasted Creevy as if he were sampling one of the region's excellent wines, calling him a Maori after the young Argentine forward had impressed him at the IRB World Junior Championship.

'"Agustín Creevy is a Maori. I want Creevy for my team in New Zealand." Hansen wanted to take him back with him to New Zealand at the age of 20,' says scrum guru Fernández Gill, who coached the Argentine under-21 side at that tournament.

Hansen, then assistant to Graham Henry, coached New Zealand under-21s in Mendoza and Creevy was a back-row forward in the host nation's side but it was as a hooker that

Hansen came across him again in 2011 when the All Blacks beat Argentina in their World Cup quarter-final in Auckland.

That was Mario Ledesma's last Pumas Test and Creevy replaced him after about an hour as he had been doing throughout the tournament, having been groomed as his successor under the tutelage of Fernández Gill.

'I trained Agustín as a young player for seven or eight years. I've known him since he was a kid. He was always a year younger than the rest in his age-group teams, he was so good.

'He was playing as number 8 in the Argentine provincial championship for Buenos Aires when we were champions three years in a row and he was one of the mainstays of that team.'

Creevy was part of Marcelo Loffreda's Pumas squad and played some early Tests as a back-row forward in 2005 and 2006. 'But he was a bit slow so we discussed turning him into a hooker. And there was his build; he was not so tall but had very long arms to bind well, but most important of all was his desire and a strong head.

'Agustín has an extraordinary mentality, he has huge faith in himself against anything and everything and he knew that playing as hooker he was going to play for the Pumas because Mario was retiring and there weren't any hookers who could overshadow him given what a brilliant player he was.

'I talked a lot with Loffreda's successor Tati Phelan about him and the idea was that he should return to Argentina to get more individual, technical training.'

Creevy was playing in France but he put his passion for the Pumas first and returned home to play for his amateur club San Luis and went on to captain the Pampas XV in the Vodacom Cup in South Africa.

'That's where he established himself as [Argentina's future] hooker, they scored lots of scrum tries and that's where he got hooked and the leap to the Pumas was automatic.

'He started training on his own. His father, a former basketball player, put up a hoop for him at home so he could practise his lineout throw.

'He was also coached by an English lineout specialist, Dan Richmond, who improved him 100 per cent as he worked with determination, throwing, I'm not exaggerating, 300 or 400 balls a day, and he practised scrummaging techniques with me and several others.

'On top of that he's an extraordinary kid, always upbeat, a leader from when he was 17. He's a natural leader.

'On the team bus he would always sit at the front by the driver with a microphone, making fun of everyone, always cheerful, a guy loved by his teammates, who shows a lot of solidarity.'

Creevy did two more years as the replacement hooker after Ledesma's retirement. He was understudy to Eusebio Guiñazú in the 2012 and 2013 Rugby Championships under Tati Phelan.

During that time he played for Montpellier where he earned another All Blacks comparison, being nicknamed 'Sonny Bill' Creevy by fans for his one-handed offloads like a seasoned back in the manner of former All Blacks centre and New Zealand rugby league player Sonny Bill Williams.

Creevy was then promoted to both first-choice hooker and captain by Daniel Hourcade in 2014 after he took charge of the Pumas. He held the Argentine caps record with 89 Tests in mid-2021, since surpassed by Nicolás Sánchez, and had captained his country in 51 of them.

He never did get the better of Hansen, though, facing and losing to the All Blacks 15 times. But he was overjoyed when he watched from afar as the Pumas beat New Zealand for the first time.

Having just moved his family to England to play for London Irish in 2020 he opted against his call-up to the squad that played in the Tri-Nations Rugby Championship in Australia later that year and made history with their first victory over the All Blacks.

He felt a big part of that victory, having captained the Pumas in five Rugby Championships and played for the Jaguares in their four Super Rugby seasons, and vowed to earn a place at a fourth World Cup in 2023.

TWENTY-NINE

MURDER

WITH THE RAVAGES of the Covid-19 pandemic just around the corner, 2020 got off to a terrible start when an incident of gratuitous violence, the result of class hatred and racism that ended in murder, had the media and large parts of Argentine society pointing the finger at rugby.

In January of that year, at the height of the summer holiday season, two separate groups of teenagers travelled to the seaside resort of Villa Gesell on the Atlantic coast south of Buenos Aires and converged, with tragic results, at a nightclub one evening.

The two groups knew nothing about each other and had never met until that night but by dawn the lives of close to a dozen boys had changed dramatically and irretrievably.

Fernando Báez Sosa, the 18-year-old son of an immigrant working-class Paraguayan couple, his father the porter at an apartment block in the capital's upmarket barrio of Recoleta, was kicked to death outside the nightclub following a heated argument inside.

The word 'rugbier' appeared in headlines reporting on Báez Sosa's death at the hands of a gang of middle-class boys aged between 18 and 20, most of them members of a rugby club in the city of Zárate, 90 kilometres north of Buenos Aires, and rugby was targeted by the media.

One of the alleged culprits was filmed kicking Báez Sosa, dazed and kneeling on the ground, in the head and screaming at him, 'Come on, you wimp, get up and fight.'

The forensic report on the victim, who had been set to study law at the University of Buenos Aires, said he had been punched in the face, arms, ribs and kidneys, and kicked in the head, causing his death by heart attack.

Investigators allege that the attack on Báez Sosa was premeditated after several boys were kicked out of the nightclub for fighting with him and his friends. Outside, they allegedly waited for Báez Sosa to come out and made sure they caught him alone, with some acting as a cordon to prevent his friends from reaching and helping him.

Eight suspects have been in prison since the murder and the case, according to media reports, had been due to go to trial some time in 2021 but was postponed until early 2023 owing to a backlog of cases in a notoriously slow judicial system. The chief culprits, should they be found guilty, face possible life imprisonment. One of the culprits had shown great promise but his dreams of playing first division rugby and, perhaps one day, for the Pumas were now shattered.

Violence

THE VAST MAJORITY of people involved in rugby find it appalling that their sport should be tainted by a case like Báez Sosa's murder. The amateur clubs throughout Argentina have always prided themselves on upholding behavioural values.

It will have hurt them to hear or read widespread criticism of a perceived elitist environment in which families encourage their sons to get into rugby because that is 'the right side of life'.

In an analysis published in the daily *Página/12*, however, a lecturer in psychology at the University of Buenos Aires wrote that these privileged boys 'disciplined' someone who 'meddled where he had no place to be'.

In the wake of the murder, the UAR and URBA recognised that rugby had tried to hide such serious issues instead of facing them head-on, says Miguel García Lombardi, and they asked him to help them.

García Lombardi comes from La Plata and played for and has trained teams at La Plata RC. He knew several of the 20 players at his club murdered by the former military regime in the 1970s and a female cousin of his was also one of the desaparecidos.

'The children of the dominant classes in La Plata took up a revolutionary stance, idealists seeking change. We were mostly upper middle class and middle class, children of professional people, there was the model of Che [Guevara], son of a doctor and a doctor himself.

'Now the composition of rugby has changed considerably; now they come from various social sectors, it's more homogenous, very positive.'

For fear of becoming another victim by association of the military regime's genocide, García Lombardi left La Plata for the southern Andean city of Bariloche in 1976, the year of the military coup.

García Lombardi returned to Buenos Aires with the return of democracy in 1983 and studied psychology, becoming a specialist in that field related to sport and eventually a go-to person when Argentine rugby faces an existentialist crisis.

He put together a plan for the URBA to address the game's behavioural issues. It was called FIMCO (Formación Integral y Mejora del Comportamiento: Comprehensive Training and Behaviour Improvement) and is divided into workshops covering players, coaches, referees and inter-club relations.

'Báez Sosa is a pivotal case; there is a before and after [Báez

Sosa]. It is rugby's problem – they are rugbiers,' García Lombardi insists.

He believes what happened to Arsenal Zárate could have happened to any club in the URBA. There was a widespread problem.

There had been two previous similar cases of an individual being killed in an attack by a group of rugby players but so far the perpetrators have escaped punishment. Coming from families with connections, they had been able to prevent the cases getting to court.

But this response by the privileged is not tolerated by Argentine society as a whole.

'There was also an incident in which five players, who were out at night in two cars, attacked two couples walking along a poorly lit road after one of the men swore at the players for driving dangerously close to them.

'One of the girls ended up in hospital. Because [allegedly] the players' families had contacts, they covered up the criminal report, paid [the victims] money and nothing happened to the kids.

'Working for traditional clubs, I have been called at least ten times in the last 20 years because of very nasty attacks by first division players that could have resulted in a death.

'I have coordinated workshops for the URBA . . . to deal with this issue [of violence] and at all the clubs they have the same story. They came within centimetres of a death, of killing someone.

'You've heard people say it: "Rugby is a man's game; we're different," so from believing ourselves better we stopped working on being better so that when these violent episodes occurred we didn't just look the other way, we brushed them under the carpet.'

As Argentine rugby has boomed over the last three decades thanks to Pumas successes, so clubs have quadrupled their playing members. This has meant the need for more coaches, the vast majority of whom are unpaid volunteers in an amateur system.

These coaches may have a deep enough knowledge of rugby to train teams from infant level to seniors on the technical aspects of the game, says García Lombardi, but they lack instruction in how to deal with mental and psychological issues, to which clubs have given a mere 5 per cent of their attention.

'There are very few of us psychologists working in [Argentine] rugby.'

The force players employ on the pitch is contained by regulations and referees but there is little effort put into ensuring players know their limits off it and do not get into punch-ups when they are out on the town after matches, and stopping some coaches from encouraging such behaviour.

'In rugby, two or more people can neutralise a single one so what's accepted in every match is that numerical superiority is valid, in fact that's what you want in defence.' So from there to ganging up on someone is only a step.

Clubs have failed to address excessive drinking and use of recreational drugs and have turned a blind eye to initiation rites known as bautismos (baptisms) that go too far into violence and abuse of new first-team players by older members of the club.

'There's systematic denial of such issues that needs addressing, and the same goes for parents, absolute minimisation of crime.

'Rugby encourages something that is really good and that is that we all work together all the time. This is of great value – it's teamwork. Now, when someone wants to fight, his teammates have to go and help him and fight no matter how and that's when you get the herd effect.

'Villa Gesell is the typical demonstration of the herd effect. The limits that prevail in individual behaviour, ethical values, inhibitors of individual violent conduct, disappear and the enemy becomes a thing to be eliminated.'

Tweets

DECADE-OLD TWEETS with discriminatory, insulting and racist comments made public right after the second of Argentina's two matches against New Zealand at the 2020 Tri-Nations Rugby Championship in Australia showed Pumas Pablo Matera, Guido Petti and Santiago Socino to have been irresponsible, narrow-minded, arrogant and racist teenagers.

The tweets were unearthed and made public – it has never been revealed by whom – to embarrass the team after a perceived inadequate show of respect for Diego Maradona following his death in Buenos Aires days before the meeting with the All Blacks.

Argentina wore black armbands for the match while New Zealand dedicated their haka to Maradona by laying an All Blacks shirt with his name and the number 10 on its back on the ground in front of the Pumas before kick-off.

Critics back home were angered by an apparent lack of recognition for Argentina's greatest sporting figure who had shown a great interest in and passion for the Pumas – as he had for all sportsmen and women in any discipline representing the country.

As a friend of Agustín Pichot, Maradona went to cheer on the Pumas at two of their matches at the 2015 World Cup in England including the semi-final against Australia.

Matera was stripped of the Pumas captaincy when the tweets came to light, a mere fortnight after he had majestically led his team to their first victory over the All Blacks.

The players' small social and rugby club circle might have fostered such attitudes of discrimination and superiority but going out into the wider world through the game, playing in Europe and for the Pumas, has broadened their minds.

Matera, Petti and Socino were suspended and ordered by the UAR to undergo a course on recognition of discrimination and racism and talk to younger players about their experiences at seminars on the subject before being allowed to be considered again for selection to the national team.

The trio publicly expressed their regret and shame for the tweets.

'It's important to say sorry when you make a mistake,' Matera told Argentina's TyC Sports. 'Those tweets surprised me as much as they did anyone who read them. I can't recall the moment when I wrote them – it really was a long time ago – but I don't want to use that as an excuse. They're in my social media and I'm responsible.

'When they went viral, I thought about everything that had happened since . . . [and] where I am today. I have changed and grown a lot, and many things have happened on the way, in my personal and professional life, in these nine years.

'Now I'm proud of where I am, the family I have, the team I'm in, the career I am making. All the good and bad things have made me the person I am today.'

The players recovered their availability to the Pumas for Test matches in 2021 but the captaincy was passed on to hooker Julián Montoya with Matera, who had worn the armband 14 times including at the 2019 World Cup, one of the first to congratulate him.

Porta criticised the UAR for having thrown the players to the wolves, believing the union hierarchy was responsible for the lack of a proper public celebration of Maradona by Argentine rugby.

THIRTY

ALL BLACKS

BEATING NEW ZEALAND became a holy grail for Argentina and it took the Pumas 24 years to get their hands on it.

It was bound to happen one day as their meetings became more frequent – twice a year almost every year from the first Rugby Championship in 2012.

Nicolás Sánchez, the only player involved in every one of Argentina's Rugby Championship campaigns that far, made it happen. He created and scored Argentina's only try and kicked all the rest of their points in a 25–15 victory cemented by a brilliant defensive performance from the Pumas.

The victory was all the more remarkable coming in Argentina's first Test match for 13 months. They had not played since beating the United States in their last World Cup pool game in Japan in October 2020.

During that time the Pumas had worked in isolation, occasionally as a squad but mostly individually given the restrictions of the Covid-19 pandemic. They no longer had the Jaguares Super Rugby franchise and their rivals had been playing in domestic Super Rugby competitions.

It was a sweet return to action for Sánchez, who had had a

disappointing World Cup and thought he might not be called up again.

'When the World Cup ended, I thought my career with the Pumas had ended. At that moment I couldn't imagine I'd be here,' Sánchez said after the Test in Sydney.

Because of Covid-19, the whole tournament was held in Australia with three teams involved in what was termed a tri-nations after reigning world champions and Rugby Championship title holders South Africa withdrew owing to restrictions posed by the pandemic.

'It's been a very hard year. After the World Cup we all felt bad, but the pandemic gave us time to dig deep and transform ourselves.'

Sánchez broke Hugo Porta's Pumas individual points record against New Zealand which had stood at 21 since he too had kicked all the points in Argentina's previous best result, a 21–21 draw in Buenos Aires in 1985.

By then Sánchez had faced New Zealand 15 times. Among other leading Pumas fly-halves, Porta played against the All Blacks seven times, Lisandro Arbizu and Felipe Contepomi six each and Juan Martín Hernández ten.

'I had an emotional exchange with Nico, thanking him and telling him two things: that I felt a part of that triumph and that that's how the Pumas' history was forged,' Porta said.

Argentina had experienced highs and lows in their half century competing with the All Blacks, from very near misses in 1985 and 2001 to a crushing 93–8 defeat in 1997.

In the amateur era, the Pumas could give the All Blacks a good game. New Zealand won a series in Buenos Aires in 1976 (21–9 and 26–6) and again when Argentina toured in 1979 (18–9 and 15–6) before the memorable series of 1985 when Porta was at his best and the first in which both nations awarded caps.

New Zealand won the first Test 33–20, in which the Argentines felt they had played better than in the second Test when they almost won.

'The draw we got against the All Blacks in 1985 was strange; I always thought we played better in the match we lost,' Porta said. 'We played dynamic, balanced, aggressive rugby with good control because we had a very clear idea of what we wanted.'

Argentina scored two tries through centre Diego Cuesta Silva and wing Juan Lanza, Porta kicked 12 points including a drop goal and they were down 15–14 at half-time.

New Zealand, who two years later would win the first World Cup and included the likes of David Kirk, Grant Fox, Andy Haden and Murray Mexted, ran in four tries, two by wing John Kirwan.

The All Blacks won the try count four-nil in the second Test with another Kirwan brace, but were stunned that they hadn't won. They had led 18–9 at the interval before Porta kicked the Pumas back into contention including a hat-trick of drop goals and Argentina would have won if number 8 Ernesto Ure had not spilt the ball when he was set to go over the line from a five-yard scrum at the death, leaving the score 21–21.

'I think [the series] was a landmark in the development of Argentine rugby. And I have no doubt that at some point the Pumas will beat the All Blacks,' Porta said after his retirement but he probably did not expect it to take another 35 years.

Argentina were within seconds of a win at the River Plate stadium in 2001 before going down 24–20 and also came tantalisingly close in their home match against New Zealand in the 2019 Rugby Championship.

The 1985 series was played at the ground of Ferro Carril Oeste, Argentine football champions in 1980 and 1982, and the Pumas would move to the stadium of another, bigger first division football club, Vélez Sarsfield, with greater capacity as they gained in popularity.

After Argentina had reached the World Cup quarter-finals in 1999 and their popularity soared, the Pumas hosted the southern hemisphere's big three teams at the giant River Plate stadium in successive seasons.

Their first match there was a 37–33 loss to South Africa in November 2000 and the third a 17–6 Australian victory in front of a record crowd for a rugby match in Argentina of 65,000 in November 2002.

New Zealand won 24–20 at River Plate with a last-gasp try in December 2001.

The All Blacks, including Jonah Lomu, Tana Umaga and a young Richie McCaw, were down 20–17 in injury time to a Pumas side they had beaten 67–19 in Christchurch six months earlier.

Playing brilliantly, Argentina scored two tries through centre Lisandro Arbizu with Felipe Contepomi kicking the other ten points.

Contepomi had a chance to find touch with a kick from behind the Argentine goalline to clinch the win but he was put under pressure by Mark Robinson and the ball veered inwards missing touch.

Andrew Mehrtens launched a counter-attack and full back Ben Blair cut between two defenders and threw a long pass to number 8 Scott Robertson who scored the winning try.

In the 2019 match at Vélez Sarsfield, the Pumas had the All Blacks on the ropes in the final minutes but failed to breach their defence from their lineout and lost 20–16.

A win might have been a good injection for the Rugby Championship and World Cup but defeat had a detrimental effect coming on the heels of the same players' loss to the Crusaders, playing as the Jaguares in the Super Rugby final in Christchurch two weeks earlier.

Argentina have come progressively closer to the All Blacks in their three World Cup meetings, losing 46–15 in 1987, 33–10 in 2011, both in New Zealand, and 26–16 at Wembley in 2015.

Pablo Matera, who captained Argentina to their first win over New Zealand, echoed Porta's sentiments when he said: 'There's a lot of people who wore this shirt before us and who fought as hard as we did to achieve this . . . I hope all of Argentine rugby felt reflected in it.'

Argentina held Australia to a 15–15 draw in Newcastle the following weekend. The Test was settled in a kicking duel between Sánchez and fellow fly-half Reece Hodge who had identical statistics, converting five of their six penalties.

Pumas coach Mario Ledesma, who had recruited his friend Michael Cheika as a consultant for the team, said the Pumas had felt emotionally and physically drained after their victory over the All Blacks.

'Fatigue affected our discipline and also the execution of our game plan but we have Nico who walks on water.

'It was always going to happen to us given the conditions in which we prepared,' he said, referring to the effects of the pandemic on their training.

Then came the third of their four matches in the tournament in which they failed to score any points as they lost 38–0 to the All Blacks, who had twice the amount of time as the Pumas to rest and prepare.

'It was the same Everest we climbed in the first match,' Ledesma said.

It was also Matera's last match as Pumas captain.

Argentina drew again with Australia in their closing match 16–16. The Wallabies fought back from a 13–6 deficit at half-time but Hodge missed a last-minute penalty.

THIRTY-ONE

CARDIFF

CARDIFF HAS WITNESSED several important moments in the history of the Pumas and one more was when secured victory in a two-Test series at the Principality Stadium in July 2021 with a 33–11 win in the second Test after drawing the first 20–20.

Argentina went into the series against Wales – who were lacking a dozen British and Irish Lions on tour in South Africa – looking to ratify their brilliant results of the previous year in the Tri-Nations Rugby Championship in Australia where they beat New Zealand for the first time and drew twice with the Wallabies.

The series, replacing an originally planned Welsh tour of Argentina, helped the present generation of Pumas to face a new reality – one similar to that which their coaching staff experienced in the first decade of the century – and show they could handle it.

No longer was the bulk of the squad based at home, the Covid pandemic having left Argentina without Super Rugby and forced the disbanding of the Jaguares, who were very nearly the sole source of Pumas. Many players sought clubs abroad, mainly in France, England and Australia.

Like more than a decade earlier, Argentina had to call up the players from a wide range of clubs in different parts of the world for a tour that started after only a few days' preparation in Bucharest. The Pumas beat Romania 24–17 but struggled for control and were far from impressed with their performance.

They moved on to Cardiff where there was considerable improvement in a 20–20 draw with Wales, playing for 50 minutes a man short after full back Juan Cruz Mallía had been sent off for a dangerous tackle. They scored two tries when down to 14 men and took a 20–6 lead but gave away two tries as the match wore on.

It was in Cardiff that the British had first taken real note of Argentina, when the Pumas visited Wales and England for the first time in 1976 and almost upset the great Welsh team of the 1970s, who had contributed strongly to one of the best Lions sides of all time, at Cardiff Arms Park.

The 1999 World Cup hosted by Wales saw Argentina reach the quarter-finals for the first time after qualifying from their pool in which they beat Samoa at Llanelli and Japan in Cardiff before upsetting Ireland in the Lens play-off.

Argentina beat Wales away for the first time in Cardiff in 2001 on a tour of Britain that also included a victory over Scotland, then held the Lions 25–25 there in 2005 and lost 27–20 in their final warm-up for the 2007 World Cup in France.

The Pumas also won in Cardiff in 2012, their first match of a tour of Europe at the end of their debut season in the Rugby Championship. Wales now lead the record with 14 wins to seven in 23 meetings including the first three for which only Argentina awarded caps.

Argentina's series-clinching win in 2021 – the fourth in a run of eight Tests with only one defeat from October 2019 to July 2021 – prepared them for the Rugby Championship less than a month later and boosted their confidence in handling their new circumstances on their way to the 2023 World Cup.

Matera and Sánchez

FLY-HALF NICOLÁS Sánchez, kicking 18 points, and flanker Pablo Matera, who celebrated his eighth Pumas try in the final minutes by vehemently booting the ball into the advertising boards behind the in-goal, have been at the heart of Argentina's drive towards the higher levels of international rugby since 2012.

Sánchez was the only player to have taken part in all their Rugby Championship campaigns while Matera, nearly five years younger, was called up for the second tournament in 2013 while playing for the Under-20s at the IRB World Junior Championship in France (renamed World Rugby Under 20 Championship from 2014). Matera would go on to amass more than 70 caps over the next eight years, while Sanchez broke former captain Agustín Creevy's record of 89 during the 2021 Rugby Championship.

To look at the statistics of that period is to see Argentina lose far more matches than they won due to the fact they were meeting only the very best teams most of the time. These streaks were punctuated by victories over the likes of Italy and Georgia and the few wins they achieved against South Africa, Australia and, eventually, New Zealand.

So, compared with an earlier period, individual player statistics look worse. For example, former captain Pedro Sporleder won 78 caps scoring 70 points from 14 tries with a record of 41 wins and 36 defeats between 1990 and 2003. The Pumas faced regional and Tier Two opposition in half of those Tests.

Sánchez, Argentina's points record holder with more than 800, had a win-loss record of 25–62 at the end of 2021 and 5–35 plus three draws in the Rugby Championship, although 6–4 in ten World Cup matches. Matera's statistics are not too different.

In regional competition Argentina had been represented for nearly a decade by their second string so the Pumas were usually measuring up only against the best teams.

The Pumas have been noted for their perseverance so their search for more wins against the best was only going to be a matter of time.

Ahead of the deciding second Test in Cardiff, these two stalwarts of the early-21st-century Pumas talked about what it meant to beat the All Blacks and the team's progress.

Sánchez: 'The World Cup was a very tough moment for all of us and I was really happy to be able to play again for the Pumas, compete again and get the chance to maybe change what we had done at the World Cup. I really thought after the World Cup that my Pumas career was over. I am grateful to Mario for the opportunity to be in the team again.'

Matera: '[Beating New Zealand] was really nice for this team whose 2019 matches, I'm not going to say were a bad experience but we hadn't achieved what we had hoped for, the team's objectives.

'So getting together again after such a long time and doing it so well, showing a different face [was good]. What had hurt us most at the World Cup was not managing to put into practice all we had prepared and not playing our best rugby and to have done that against New Zealand and on top of that with the victory as a consequence was great.

'Argentine rugby had been growing a lot since our inclusion in the Rugby Championship and Super Rugby, making big forward strides. But after what happened in 2020, with the Jaguares disappearing after all the great effort put in by a lot of people who had committed themselves to the franchise, and players suddenly having to go out and look for clubs in France, England, Australia to continue with their professional careers, there was big a step back.

'So achieving what had never been done before was to take more steps forward and show that the Argentine team keeps growing in different conditions, now all separated, having been easier when we were all together.'

Sánchez: 'It was a historic victory and to beat New Zealand

was also to validate something very important which is all we'd been working for and the whole culture of hard work we want to create and feeling we're on the right track.'

A major difficulty faced by Argentina had often been maintaining a lead against top opponents and managing tactically to secure a win, coping with the final quarter when the benches, or finishers, often change the course of a game.

Matera: 'I think it's down to experience, knowing how to close out matches, knowing how to play against teams that maybe we used to think we couldn't beat and today we can play them on level terms. In fact, our last two matches against Australia, we drew them both playing there; I think that's experience.

'As Nico said, validating the whole process of what we're doing as a team, which is very hard when there aren't any results, because you're on a path and you've got to keep believing it's the right one and when results don't come with it, it gets complicated. I think that since that [victory over New Zealand] the team is better prepared to play against those top teams.

'Looking at our last match (20–20 against Wales), a few years back if we'd had a red card it would surely have been 99 per cent lost – there was no way of winning it – yet the other day we played as equals with Wales with a man less and that shows the team's maturity.'

Another World Cup in France brings back memories of Argentina's best performance on the international stage in 2007 when most of the Pumas' squad were exiles. The coaching staff preparing the team for 2023 were part of that achievement.

Matera: 'It's what we have been dealt and we try to get the best out of the conditions as they are. Of course, there are positive things: we miss each other a lot more, we love getting together, month-long tours like this one fly by. Before we were used to being together all year.

'Some of the players have played with the staff, Nico for instance with Mario (Ledesma) at the 2011 World Cup. I played alongside Corcho (Juan Fernández Lobbe), we all feel the same thing for this shirt. They understand what it is to be on our [players'] side so I think that has produced something really nice in the team.'

Both Matera and Sánchez play for Stade Français in Paris so the subject of 2007 might be part of changing-room banter with their French teammates, or the last time the teams met when France won their pool match in Japan in 2019.

Matera: 'There is more talk of what happened the last time when we lost. Now we don't know if we're going to meet but it's good that a large part of our team are playing in France with the World Cup there.'

THIRTY-TWO

OLYMPICS

ARGENTINA'S SEVENS PLAYERS are also Pumas, driven by the same passion as their counterparts in the 15-man game to which many of them progress.

Their team's bronze medal at the 2020 Olympic Games, held in Tokyo in 2021 due to the Covid-19 pandemic, was ultimately down to the work of coach Santiago 'Coyote' Gómez Cora since 2013.

The players overcame seemingly insurmountable odds in their quarter-final against South Africa, bronze medal winners at Rio 2016, when veteran Gastón Revol was sent off after two minutes for a neck-high tackle.

Argentina were down 7–0 at the time but fought back to lead 14–7 at half-time and 19–7 early in the second half. Where South Africa would have expected to find gaps in a side a man short it was the very fast and elusive Marcos Moneta finding them in the Springboks. Argentina won 19–14.

Gómez Cora, who until 2016 held the world record for most tries in sevens rugby with 230, has been involved in many of Argentina's highlights, as player and coach, on the world circuit.

He was part of the team that reached the 2009 Sevens World

Cup final in Dubai where they lost to Wales – having beaten them in the group stage.

Long before that, in 2001, Argentina hosted the third Sevens World Cup at Mar del Plata on the Atlantic coast and reached the semi-finals with a side that included Agustín Pichot, Felipe Contepomi, Nani Corleto, Tati Phelan and Diego Albanese.

Given the job of coaching the Pumas Sevens, Gómez Cora prepared them for rugby's return to the Olympics in 2016 in Rio de Janeiro where they lost a nerve-wracking quarter-final to Great Britain 5–0 in sudden-death extra time having missed a last-gasp kick at the posts at the end of normal time.

That side was strengthened by two players who had reached the 2015 Rugby World Cup semi-finals with the Pumas, three-quarters Juan Imhoff and Matías Moroni.

The team that beat Great Britain 17–12 in the bronze medal match in Tokyo was a fine balance of experience and youth with seven veterans of the Pan American Games gold medal in Lima in 2019 including the 34-year-old Revol, and three young players who had helped the country win gold at the Youth Olympic Games in Buenos Aires in 2018. Among these was the fast and elusive Moneta who top-scored with six tries in the tournament and was later voted world sevens player of the year.

The only sides Argentina lost to were the finalists: New Zealand, in their pool, and champions Fiji, who retained their title, in the semi-finals.

GLOSSARY

Rugbier

The English language, strangely given its richness of vocabulary, has no single word for a rugby player or player of many sports like tennis, hockey or polo to name others that Argentines excel at – only footballer.

In Spanish he/she is a *futbolista* and the rugby equivalent is a *rugbista* but Argentines found the perfect term for themselves with an English touch: rugbier.

It has so pervaded the Argentine lexicon that it describes more than just a man or woman who plays rugby but also a person associated with the sport and the communities that play it.

La bajadita

A scrum formation patented by Argentina in which the pack binds very low and all eight forwards push in unison to move the opposing pack off the ball. The name, diminutive of *bajada*, comes from *bajar*, to go down. (The J is pronounced like a guttural H.)

Tercer tiempo

In Spanish sports terminology the word *tiempo* (time) is the equivalent to half in English and the 'third half' of a match is the traditional post-match get-together with opponents for drinks and/or dinner, a very important part of Argentine club rugby.

Biei (beeay)

Phonetic spelling in Spanish of BA, the term used to refer to Buenos Aires Cricket & Rugby Club, whose official foundation year as Buenos Aires Football Club is 1864 although it had been in existence for longer. It changed to BACRC when it merged with the older BA Cricket Club in 1951.

In 1899, it became one of the five clubs that formed the River Plate Rugby Championship, predecessor of the Unión Argentina de Rugby. The others were Rosario Athletic (1867), Lomas Athletic (1891), Flores Athletic (1893) and Belgrano Athletic (1896). All but Flores are still active today in top-flight domestic rugby.

Acronyms and other names

CASI: Club Atlético San Isidro (commonly Casi)
SIC: San Isidro Club (Sic)
CUBA: Club Universitario de Buenos Aires (Cuba)
Plaza: Nickname of Atlético del Rosario, after its Plaza Jewell ground
UAR: Unión Argentina de Rugby (Uar)
FUAR: Fundación de la UAR (Fuar)
URBA: Unión de Rugby de Buenos Aires (Urba)
UCR: Unión Cordobesa de Rugby (Córdoba)
URT: Unión de Rugby de Tucumán
URR: Unión de Rugby de Rosario
URC: Unión de Rugby de Cuyo (originally Mendoza and San Juan, now only Mendoza)
PladAR: Plan de Desarrollo y Alto Rendimiento (Development and High Performance Plan)
SLAR: Super Liga Americana de Rugby (South American Super Rugby)

Team names

International:
Los Pumas – Senior national team
Pumitas (little Pumas) or M20 (menores de 20 = younger than or under 20)
Argentina XV – second string/development side
Jaguares – Super Rugby franchise
Jaguares XV – second string franchise in SLAR

Pampas XV – development team

Jaguars (in English) or Sudamérica XV – South America XV

Provincial:

Naranja (orange) – Tucumán

Dogos (Argentine breed of dog) – Córdoba

Ñandúes (rheas) – Rosario

Guanacos (relative of llama) – Cuyo (Mendoza)

Nicknames

Their nicknames are what many people involved in Argentine rugby are known by, from shortened, abbreviated or diminutive versions of their first names, Agus for Agustín, Liso for Lisandro, or surnames, Legui for Leguizamón, to descriptive names like Huevo (egg).

Tito, which is a diminutive like Juancito: Little John, is the name the players gave Izak van Heerden, a big South African who coached the 1965 Pumas.

Among the Pumas, there are Pochola Silva, Gato (cat) Handley, Tano (Italian) Loffreda, Tati (Santiago) Phelan, Corcho (cork) Fernández Lobbe, Toro (bull) Ayerza, Cachorro (puppy) Sánchez.

A chance meeting that could be said to have been filthy brought together three players from different clubs who answered to the names Asco (repulsive), Basura (rubbish) and Caca (poo).

But such nicknames, which lots of players including the 'victims' would find amusing but others might find hurtful and offensive, are being discouraged as rugby tries to clean up its behaviour.

Note for English speakers

Words ending in E take an accent in Spanish when the emphasis is on the end of a word like yaguareté, the animal on the Pumas badge, but not on mate, the tea indigenous to Paraguay, Uruguay and northern Argentina because the emphasis is on the first syllable, MA. There is a tendency in English copy to put an accent on mate so readers are aware it is pronounced mahteh, likewise yaguareté: jaguarehteh. So a name like Albacete doesn't take an accent but the final E is pronounced, and Hourcade, although a French name, is oorcahdeh.

World Cup record

1987 – pool phase: one win, two defeats
1991 – pool phase: three defeats
1995 – pool phase: three defeats
1999 – quarter-finals: three wins, two defeats
2003 – pool phase: two wins, two defeats
2007 – third place: six wins, one defeat
2011 – quarter-finals: three wins, two defeats
2015 – semi-finals: four wins, three defeats
2019 – pool phase: two wins, two defeats

Rugby Championship record

(normally 6 Tests, 3 in World Cup years)
2012 – 4th: 4 points (1 draw, 2 bonus)
2013 – 4th: 2 points (2 bonus)
2014 – 4th: 7 points (1 win, 3 bonus)
2015 (3 Tests) – 3rd: 5 points (1 win, 1 bonus)
2016 – 4th: 5 points (1 win, 1 bonus)
2017 – 4th: 0 points
2018 – 4th: 8 points (2 wins)
2019 (3 Tests) – 4th: 2 points (2 bonus)
2020 (4 Tests) – 2nd: 8 points (1 win, 2 draws)
2021 (6 Tests) – 4th: 0 points

Best Sevens results

2001 World Cup semi-finals
2009 World Cup runners-up
2020 Olympic Games bronze medal

ACKNOWLEDGEMENTS

———————————— 🐾 ————————————

This book is dedicated to the memory of my English father, Gerry Gowar – who captained 'Biei' (Buenos Aires Cricket & Rugby Club) in 1941 and sat me on his shoulders to watch my first rugby matches behind the perimeter fence at CASI in the 1950s – and my late younger brother Chris, a talented centre.

My thanks go to my Argentine, British, French and southern hemisphere colleagues.Shared experiences, big or small, all contributed to this book.

Special thanks to Jorge Búsico, *La Nación* rugby columnist and author of *Ser Puma* (*To be a Puma*) and *El Rugido* (*The Roar*), for his help and encouragement in long chats about the Argentine game and its leading lights.

Also to Frankie Deges, a 'Biei' stalwart and the first touring Pumas press officer, former *BA Herald* sports editor Eric Weil and 'Hugo' Davies, who gave me my first job in sports journalism as a freelance Argentina football correspondent in 1977.

A special mention for the late UAR treasurer Carlos Barbieri, who sadly died so soon after making his contribution to the book, and the great loose forward and Pumas captain Hector 'Pochola' Silva, who also passed away in 2021.

Thanks above all to the players, coaches and officials who talked to me about the parts they played in Pumas history and so many others I didn't speak with who wore the sky blue and white shirt with pride.

BIBLIOGRAPHY

Ser Puma, Jorge Búsico, Pablo Mamone, Alejandro Cloppet

Los Pumas, Ezequiel Fernández Moores, Andrés Vilegas, preface by Hugo Mackern

Pochola Silva, Pasión y Coraje, Héctor Silva

El Rugido, Jorge Búsico

El Juego Manda, Agustín Pichot

Rugby Didáctico 4, Espíritu y filosofía, Sebastián Perasso

Veco Villegas, Pasión por el Rugby, Sebastián Perasso

Rugby: The Art of Scrummaging, Enrique 'Topo' Rodríguez

Maten al Rugbier, Claudio Gómez

El Clan Puccio, Rodolfo Palacios

Archive material from *El Gráfico*, *La Nación*, *Clarín*, *Buenos Aires Herald*, *infobae*, *Página 12*, *The Times* and *Sunday Times*, *Guardian*, *Observer*, *Telegraph*, *Reuters*, *Rugby World*, *L'Equipe*, *Midi Olympique*, club websites, match programmes, rugbypass. com, aplenorugby.com.ar, ESPN statistics (Argentina results, points, caps) and 'Revolución Puma'.

Personal archive.